THE HOME BUILDERS

Embracing the Art of the Home

PROVERBS 24: 3-4

DONNA GAINES // MARGE LENOW
JEAN STOCKDALE // DAYNA STREET
ANGIE WILSON

CONTENTS

HOW TO USE THIS STUDY

The moral fabric of the home is under siege. Contrary to secular distortion, our homes are to be faith shapers that extend love and encouragement, uphold truth, value holiness, and teach righteousness. *The Home Builders: Embracing the Art of the Home* is a twelve-week study based upon the wisdom and insight of Proverbs 24:3-4 that utilizes scriptural principles and practical tips to challenge women in every season of life to embrace the ministry of the home.

This study is designed to provide an opportunity for personal study throughout the week leading up to a small group discussion and large group teaching time once a week. Each session is divided into five daily homework assignments and provides Bible study and personal application with room for notes.

In your small group time each week, you will be able to connect with other women and build "iron sharpening iron" relationships. As you come together, be ready to share what God has shown you through His Word using the weekly studies as a guide. In the large group teaching time, you will be challenged by relevant, biblical instruction that will encourage you to build your home upon a solid foundation, the Word of God.

> *Therefore everyone who hears these words of Mine and acts on them, may be compared to a wise man who built his house on the rock. And the rain fell, and the floods came, and the winds blew and slammed against that house; and yet it did not fall, for it had been founded on the rock.*
>
> Matthew 7:24-25

Week 1
INTRODUCTION

By wisdom a house is built, and by understanding it is established;
And by knowledge the rooms are filled with all precious and pleasant riches.
Proverbs 24:3-4

Birds have it. As do whales, turtles, cats, and snails. A homing instinct. Smells and sounds pair up with an internal compass and draw these animals home. Humans are no different. While we may not have a homing compass, we are all born with a desire for home. Where did the prodigal son run when he found himself eating with the pigs? Home. Where do we want to go at the end of a tough day? Home.

So what is it that calls us home? It is more than comfort and familiarity. What draws us home is love, acceptance, warmth, and a sense of belonging. As Sally Clarkson writes,

> We pine to belong to a place in which our story began, where the stories of others intertwine with ours in a history that sustains us through dark nights and winter seasons, where our loneliness can be comforted and we can encounter the affection of God and human alike... We want a refuge that is more than a house, with rooms that speak to us with a living presence and enwrap us with welcome when we return. We hunger for the rich community of love, the family that ought to fill those rooms.[1]

There is no place like home. But, in recent years, the home has been increasingly under assault and as Clarkson notes, "Many in our time have never known home at all, in the sense of something more than a collections of rooms...and few of us have any real sense of a local community or history."[2]

Instability has become a pandemic in our society. For the most part, permanence and stability are notions of the past. Gone are the days when most people worked for the same company for their entire career. Urbanization has devoured one small town after another as families migrate by the droves to metropolitan areas looking for what they think is a better life. Layers of extended family that once provided stability have been stripped away by increasing divorce rates and frequent job relocations. The word "neighbor" is becoming an antiquated term as most families live in houses with revolving doors next door to people they don't know or care to know because neither will be there long.

Stability is prized, however, by Christian communities. Since the sixth century, a vow of stability has been a requirement for those who would follow in the Benedictine tradition:

We live together, pray together, work together, relax together. We give up the temptation to move from place to place in search of an ideal situation. Ultimately there is no escape from oneself, and the idea that things would be better someplace else is usually an illusion. And when interpersonal conflicts arise, we have a great incentive to work things out and restore peace. This means learning the practices of love: acknowledging one's own offensive behavior, giving up one's preferences, forgiving.[3]

By taking this vow, one order notes they resist "all temptation to escape the truth about ourselves."[4] This embracement of stability stands in stark contrast to the instability upon which our postmodern culture thrives.

What is stability? The Merriam-Webster Dictionary defines *stability* as "the property of a body that causes it when disturbed from a condition of equilibrium or steady motion to develop forces or moments that restore the original condition."[5] Isn't that something we all desire? A place of restoration that provides balance.

Edith Schaeffer wisely observed:

> Human beings are very unbalanced and prone to go off on tangents. In every area of life—with too great emphasis on one thing, leaving out another important thing altogether. None of us will ever be perfectly balanced in our spiritual lives, our intellectual lives, our emotional lives, our family lives, in relationships with other human beings, or in our business lives. BUT WE ARE CHALLENGED TO TRY, WITH THE HELP OF GOD. We are meant to live in the scriptures.[6]

So, where is that place of stability that returns us to equilibrium, the place where we can be challenged to live in the Scriptures and before the face of God? From the beginning, God ordained that place to be the home. Homes are to be faith shapers that extend love and encouragement, uphold truth, value holiness, and teach righteousness. Homes are to be sacred dwellings, equipping stations, and evangelistic outposts. Homes are refuges for rest and renewal.

But sadly, we are living in an increasingly homeless generation. Not homeless as in those who do not have structural housing, but homeless as in those who do not live in a stable, restorative place of amazing grace built upon the foundation of God's Word.

The need for home—for true stability—is greater than ever. Consequently, never has there been a greater need for women, all women—single, married, widowed, in all seasons and phases of life—to have the godly *wisdom* to skillfully build stable homes, the *understanding* to securely establish them on a righteous foundation, and the *knowledge* needed to fill up the rooms of our homes with what God's Word says are precious and pleasant riches.

So, where do we begin? With ourselves. As C.S. Lewis proposed:

> Imagine yourself as a living house. God comes in to rebuild that house. At first, perhaps, you can understand what He is doing. He is getting the drains right and stopping the leaks in the roof and so on; you knew that those jobs needed doing and so you are not surprised. But presently He starts knocking the house about in a way that hurts abominably and does not seem to make any sense. What on earth is He up to? The explanation is that He is building quite a different house from the one you thought of—throwing out a new wing here, putting on an extra floor there, running up towers, making courtyards. You thought you were being made into a decent little cottage: but He is building a palace.[7]

Before we can make a home for others, God must make His home in us. The task ahead is two-fold. Before God can build *through* us, He will ready us by doing a transforming work *in* us. Only God can take a rough cabin in disrepair and transform it into a grand palace by saturating it with His truth.

Our journey forward is a soulful work, a redemptive work, a holy work. We cannot create stable, restorative homes on our own. As the Psalmist warned, "Unless the Lord builds the house, they labor in vain who build it" (Psalm 127:1). And when He builds His home in us and through us, the result will be an eternal influence that will outlast our lifetime.

Week 2
WISDOM

Through [skillful and godly] wisdom a house [a life, a home, a family] is built,
and by understanding it is established [on a sound and good foundation].
Proverbs 24:3 AMP

All of us desire wisdom. James tells us that God desires to provide it if we will only ask (James 1:5). Wisdom is the foundation upon which our lives and homes should be built. Because God created the world by His wisdom and in His order, we need to seek His counsel for living according to His plan. He has revealed His plan for life in His Word.

Wisdom is defined as: "knowledge, experience, intelligence; and all wisdom has its source in Him."[8] Jesus is the ultimate revelation of the wisdom of God and the Rock that undergirds our lives and our homes enabling us to stand against the storms of life (Matthew 7:24-27).

We all face situations in life, marriage, family, work or relationships where we need wisdom. God has given us the principles for living in His Word. As we look at what the Bible has to say about wisdom, you will be laying a foundation upon which your family can be established.

DAY ONE

"The fear of the Lord is the beginning of wisdom" (Proverbs 9:10). Since it is the beginning of our study, we would do well to start there.

1. Read the following verses and summarize what you learn about the fear of the Lord.

    Deuteronomy 6:2

    Deuteronomy 8:6

    Deuteronomy 31:12

God told the Israelites to place the 12 stones from the Jordan as a memorial to the Lord. It was to be a reminder of how God had moved on their behalf. They were to tell their children about the might of the Lord so that they might fear the Lord forever.

Do you ever share your testimony with your children or grandchildren? What about a recent answer to prayer or a way the Lord has spoken to you through His Word? Remembering boosts our faith. Passing on the testimonies of God's goodness and might on our behalf teaches our children to fear the Lord and to obey Him.

2. Write out a personal testimony of recent answered prayer below and then share it with one of your children or grandchildren.

    Who did you share it with?

3. Read 1 Samuel 12:14-15. These words were spoken through Samuel when Saul was made king. Obedience to God's commands is the result of fearing the Lord. What are the consequences if we don't fear the Lord?

4. Read 2 Kings 17:34-39. Once again we see the Lord commanding His people not to fear the gods of the nations around them but only the One True Living God. What promise does God give His people if they will fear Him and obey His commands?

The remarkable thing about God is that when you fear God, you fear nothing else, whereas if you do not fear God, you fear everything else.[9] — Oswald Chambers

5. Look up 2 Chronicles 19:7 and Job 28:28. According to these verses, what is the opposite of fearing the Lord?

6. Read Psalm 36:1. What happens to those who do not fear the Lord?

As we close out our study today, take a few moments to consider this observation on Psalm 36:1 from A. W. Tozer:

> When the psalmist saw the transgression of the wicked his heart told him how it could be. 'There is no fear of God before his eyes,' he explained, and in so saying revealed to us the psychology of sin. When men no longer fear God, they transgress His laws without hesitation. The fear of consequences is no deterrent when the fear of God is gone. In olden days men of faith were said to 'walk in the fear of God' and to 'serve the Lord with fear.' However intimate their communion with God, however bold their prayers, at the base of their religious life was the conception of God as awesome and dreadful....
>
> Wherever God appeared to men in the Bible times the results were the same — an overwhelming sense of terror and dismay, a wrenching sensation of sinfulness and guilt. When God spoke, Abram stretched himself upon the ground to listen. When Moses saw the Lord in the burning bush he hid his face in fear to look upon God. Isaiah's vision of God wrung from him the cry, 'Woe is me!' and the confession, 'I am undone; because I am a man of unclean lips.'[10]

DAY TWO

God blesses obedience. Unless we have a reverential fear (awe) of God, we will not obey His Word. As I explained in *Choose Wisely, Live Fully,*

> This desire to obey leads to further revelation and understanding. The path of life grows brighter and brighter as we continue to choose God's way instead of our own (Proverbs 4:18)…It is through wholehearted devotion to Him that life begins to make sense, and you are allowed to 'see' what had been veiled before. God is good. He desires to bless His children. When the Bible uses the word blessed it can also be translated 'happy'. You will not find true happiness apart from Christ.[11]

For years, I have made it a practice to pray many of the blessings in Scripture for my family. Psalm 112:1-2 are two verses I have in my prayer notebook. I was recently talking to one of my daughters and the Lord had directed her to these two verses. The entire Psalm is one of encouragement. Why don't you add these verses to your prayer notebook or journal and begin to pray them for your family?

> Praise the Lord! How blessed is the man who fears the Lord,
> Who greatly delights in His commandments.
> His descendants will be mighty on earth;
> The generation of the upright will be blessed.
>
> Psalm 112:1-2

1. Look up the following scriptures and make a list of the blessings associated with the fear of the Lord. Choose at least two of these to pray for your family.

Psalm 25:14

Psalm 33:18

Psalm 34:7

Psalm 103:17

Psalm 128:1

Proverbs 10:27

Proverbs 14:26-27

Proverbs 15:33

Proverbs 19:23

Proverbs 22:4

2. Review the list of blessings you have just finished compiling. As you reflect on them, ask the Lord to show you any area of rebellion in your own life. Is there an area that you are having difficulty dedicating to the Lord?

Our rebellion and leaning on our own understanding leads to frustration and discouragement. Repent and ask the Lord to allow the fear of Him to lead you to obedience and blessing.

FIXER UPPER

We have always been intentional about having Scripture visible in our home. It can be art on the wall or a framed verse on a side table. Inventory your rooms and pray about specific scriptures with which you would like to fill your home.

DAY THREE

When I think of wise women in Scripture, my mind automatically goes to Deborah. She is one of my favorite women in the Bible. Her story is recorded in Judges 4-5. She lived during the time of the Judges after the conquest of the Promised Land, but before Israel was ruled by the kings. This period of approximately 300-400 years was marked by sin cycles. Israel would experience peace when a judge ruled them. But after the death of the judge, the people would return to pagan idolatry and the Lord would allow one of the pagan nations around them to oppress them.

Deborah judged in Israel after Ehud and Shamgar. Once again, the Israelites had committed evil in the eyes of the Lord and God allowed the Canaanites and their King Jabin to oppress them.

1. Read Judges 4:1-3. How long had the people been living in oppression?

The people cried out to the Lord and He heard them. He sent His message through a faithful woman who, according to the Bible (Judges 4:4), was a prophetess judging Israel at the time. Deborah was the fourth judge of Israel. The ESV Study Bible points out that, "Deborah's actions and words consistently pointed to God, not away from him, in contrast to the poor choices of judges like Gideon, Jephthath, and Samson."[12]

Deborah was a woman who feared the Lord and was sought out for her wisdom.

2. Read Judges 4:4-10. What message did God give through Deborah?

3. How did Barak respond?

4. What does this tell you about his respect for Deborah?

One biographer notes,

> We can imagine that Deborah looked the part of a great and noble woman. She must have had fire in her eyes, determination in her step, and a positive ring to her voice. We can see her, a tall, handsome woman, wearing a dress of blue striped in red and yellow and a yellow turban with a long, pure-white cotton veil, lace edged, reaching to the hem of her dress. A feminine woman, who never had the ambition to push herself forward, Deborah better personified the homemaker in Israel than a warrior. But as she counseled with her people and began to sense their common danger, she kindled in them an enthusiasm for immediate action against the enemy.[13]

When Sisera, the commander of Jabin's army, heard that Barak had gone to Mt. Tabor to go to battle with him, he called together all of his chariots and men. The Bible tells us in Judges 4:15 that the Lord routed Sisera and his army. Sisera fled on foot with Barak pursuing him.

5. Read Judges 4:17-24. What happened to Sisera? Who did God lead him to and how was he killed?

6. Did God fulfill His Word through Deborah?

7. Read Judges 5:6-7. When Deborah arose what happened?

Judges 5 tells us that life in the Israelite villages had all but ceased. There was no business taking place and the elders were unable to serve at the gates of the city. Terror had filled their land. Does that sound familiar? But there was a woman who believed God. She simply took Him at His Word and the Lord used her to impact history and bring relief and peace to His people.

How are you allowing God to use you to make a difference?

DAY FOUR

The Bible says, "Righteousness exalts a nation, but sin is a disgrace to any people" (Proverbs 14:34). Under the righteous leadership of Deborah, God intervened on behalf of His people.

Read Judges 4-5.

1. How were the Israelites exalted when they had righteous leaders?

2. What does the Bible tell us about Deborah?

3. She led Israel in four distinct ways. List them:

   a.

   b.

   c.

   d.

5. Deborah and Barak sang a song of victory. What other woman in Scripture led the Israelites in a victory song?

It is important for us to make connections as we work through scripture. God often works in different ways on behalf of His people but He will never contradict His Word or His character.

6. How did God fight against Sisera and his chariots? (Judges 5:4-5 & 20-21).

In their book, *Women of Awakenings*, Lewis and Betty Drummond note,

> Not only was Sisera slain, Canaan was subdued, and Jabin with it. The Scriptural account tells us that "the hands of the sons of Israel pressed heavier and heavier upon Jabin, the King of Canaan" (Judges 4:24). When God gives victory, He gives full victory; when God revives His people, He revives them thoroughly; when God defeats evil, He eradicates it victoriously. And it all came about because of this woman of awakening.[14]

7. How long did the land have rest after this victory?

The description of terror that filled the land because of the oppression of the Canaanites makes me think about the day in which we live and the threat of terror from Isis and other forces hostile to Christianity. What we need are men and women of God who will stand firm against the schemes of the evil one (Ephesians 6:10-12). God will use wise women who revere the Lord to have the power to push back the darkness and advance the Kingdom of God. All it takes to be a Deborah is to simply walk with God and say, "yes" to His will.

DAY FIVE

John Ortberg said in *The Life You've Always Wanted,* "We have largely traded wisdom for information, depth for breadth. We want to microwave maturity."[15] There is no way to "fast track" yourself to maturity or to speed up the process. Just as it takes time for a baby to grow into an adult, it takes time for a new Christian to grow into a wise man or woman. Wisdom is the result of faithfully choosing to obey God's Word and to believe Him. As you do, God will reveal Himself to you and you will begin to "see" how He desires to use your life.

I admire so many of the women in Scripture. But I have also enjoyed studying women from history. Last summer I read a book by Eric Metaxas titled, *Seven Women.* He wrote a brief biography about seven women who were used by God to change their culture and impact the world for Christ. These were ordinary women who believed, loved and lived for an extraordinary God. The seven he chose were: Joan of Arc, Susanna Wesley (who we will look at briefly in our chapter on Prayer), Hannah More, Saint Maria of Paris, Corrie Ten Boom, Rosa Parks, and Mother Teresa.

I want to introduce you to Hannah More. Hannah lived in England (1745-1833). She was according to Metaxas, "The most influential woman of her time."[16] She was a best-selling playwright and author, whose father was an educator. Her extraordinary skill allowed her to be catapulted into the circles of the elite in London. It would be through these connections that she would meet William Wilberforce and the two would join forces to abolish slavery.

Hannah More also befriended John Newton, the former slave trader who embraced Christianity and had a profound impact upon William Wilberforce. Newton was a minister in the Church of England and wrote the hymn, *Amazing Grace.* In fact, it was Newton's advice that caused Wilberforce to stay in politics and allow God to use him there.

Wilberforce, Newton, and More led the fight against the slave trade and won by educating the people about the evils of slavery, much of which was done through More's writing. Parliament voted to abolish slavery just weeks before More's death.

I admire Hannah More's devotion and dedication to the Lord and to the poor and mistreated. Not only did she fight for the end of the slave trade, she also started schools for the coal miner's children. Their "Sunday Schools" (so named because they met on Sunday when the children were not working) were held to teach the poorest children how to read. She stated that, "Education, specifically in religion, would go a long way toward lifting these people out of the morass of hopelessness and criminality so rampant among them...By the 1850s, 75 percent of all laboring-class children between five and fifteen were enrolled in Sunday Schools."[17]

The other woman in Metaxas' book who captured my heart was Rosa Parks. Parks lived from 1913-2005. She is affectionately remembered as the "Mother of the Civil Rights Movement."[18] You probably remember her as the woman who refused to give up her seat on a bus. "This simple act launched the year-long Montgomery bus boycott, which in turn catapulted Martin Luther King Jr. to fame and effectively set in motion the Civil Rights Movement."[19]

Rosa Parks was a shy, dignified, Christian woman. She worked hard and was involved with her husband in civil rights issues. Because she was black, she lived with the horrendous indignities of the Jim Crow South. She lived in the era of "separate drinking fountains, separate restrooms, and separate elevators."[20] My heart broke as I read her story and realized, her story is the same as so many of the African Americans who lived in the South during the 1900's.

Rosa Parks's refusal to get up from her seat soon received national attention. In fact, her arrest and subsequent trials led to the Supreme Court decision on November 13, 1956, that declared it unconstitutional to segregate buses. The passage of the 1964 Civil Rights Act was a victory Parks celebrated. She later published her autobiography and a second book, *Quiet Strength*. It was this book that revealed "how great a role Rosa's faith in God played through her long life and through her struggles. 'As a child I learned from the Bible to trust in God and not be afraid', Rosa wrote. And 'I felt the Lord would give me the strength to endure whatever I had to face. God did away with all my fear.'"[21]

Rosa Parks was granted many awards. She flew to Sweden in 1994 to accept "the Rosa Parks Peace Prize. In 1996, President Clinton awarded her the Presidential Medal of Freedom; in 1999 the U. S. Congress awarded Rosa the Congressional Gold Medal. *Time* magazine named Rosa Parks 'one of the twenty most influential and iconic figures of the twentieth century.'"[22] I am so grateful for Rosa. She understood because of her faith in God, that all people are created in His image and had dignity and worth. Consequently, there is only one race – the human race.

These influential women who are greatly revered by us today, were wise women who placed their trust in God. Faith and fear cannot coexist in the human heart. These women chose faith over fear and stood against injustice and God used them to challenge the status quo, awaken nations to change and advance the gospel of Jesus Christ. They were women just like you and me. Ordinary women serving their extraordinary God and living to see what only He can do. Will you join their ranks? All it takes is saying "no" to fear and "yes" to faith. Believe and be used by God!

1. It is so important that we fill the rooms of our homes with the faith and character of these women. Which one of them has spoken to or challenged you?

2. How will you conquer fear in your own life and choose to live for Christ and the gospel?

3. What daily practices will you incorporate into your life that will help you mature and become a wise woman?

It only takes one woman surrendered to God to speak truth to a dark and hurting world, just like our sisters in Christ have done throughout the centuries. Pray and believe. Then obey and see what God will do!

We have so much to learn from these wise women. I encourage you to read Christian biographies and fill your homes with these treasures. Introduce your children to the great people of faith.

Here are a few that I would recommend:

50 People Every Christian Should Know by Warren Wiersbe

A Chance to Die: The Life and Legacy of Amy Carmichael by Elisabeth Elliott

Dream Big: The Henrietta Mears Story, Editor Earl O. Roe

Fierce Convictions: The Extraordinary Life of Hannah More: Poet, Reformer, Abolitionist by Karen Swallow Prior

Kisses From Katie by Katie Davis (autobiographical)

Marriage to a Difficult Man: The Uncommon Union of Jonathan and Sarah Edwards by Elisabeth Dodds

Seven Women by Eric Metaxas

The Hiding Place by Corrie ten Boom (autobiography)

Women of Awakenings by Lewis and Betty Drummond

Week 3
UNDERSTANDING

For this reason also, since the day we heard of it, we have not ceased to pray for you and to ask that you may be filled with the knowledge of His will in all spiritual wisdom and understanding, so that you will walk in a manner worthy of the Lord, to please Him in all respects, bearing fruit in every good work and increasing in the knowledge of God; strengthened with all power, according to His glorious might, for the attaining of all steadfastness and patience; joyously giving thanks to the Father, who has qualified us to share in the inheritance of the saints in Light.

Colossians 1:9-12

Proverbs 24:3-4 says, "By wisdom a house is built, and by understanding it is established." We are digging into the topic of "understanding" this week. The biblical concept of understanding transcends gathering facts and finds its source in the person of God and in the Word of God. Biblical understanding is the ability to discern and gain clarity through the filter of God's Word, turning information into revelation.

As R.C. Sproul notes, "Our Lord calls for a continued application of the mind to His Word. A disciple does not dabble in learning. He makes the pursuit of an understanding of God's Word a chief business of his life."[23]

DAY ONE

The Bible seems to use the words "knowledge," "understanding," and "wisdom" almost interchangeably. These three key words are often linked together and closely associated.

1.   Read Proverbs 9:10. Write out this verse. Describe how our three key words are used in this verse.

A closer look at these three biblical terms reveals distinct meanings. Knowledge is the accumulation and familiarization of truth gained from the systematic study of God's Word and/or information through experience, reasoning, or acquaintance. Understanding is the ability to gather meaning from the facts in order to develop personal convictions from biblical principles as the framework for living a holy and sanctified life. Wisdom, in the simplest term, is the practical application of biblical knowledge and understanding in a given context that results in a course of action to ultimately honor the Lord.

Prior to conversion, we operated in the realm of the five senses which are sight, hearing, taste, smell, and touch. This behavior generally produced a natural wisdom, understanding, and knowledge. Having come to Christ for salvation, we have been given the indwelling Spirit of God as our internal control and the Word of God as our external control. No longer are we compelled to operate through our natural resources.

2. Read Psalm 119:130. What is required of us in order to live in truth?

While we are pursing personal holiness and practical righteousness, we will need to become students of God's Word. Sadly, it is possible to have knowledge of Bible facts, but lack understanding and wisdom.

3. Read Proverbs 4:7. What is necessary for us to gain wisdom?

As believers we need to glean biblical truth, apply understanding under the Spirit's leading, and act in wisdom in order to operate in the realm of the abundant life in Christ. In doing so, we will live in a way that honors and glorifies Jesus. A fruitful life for Christ is (should be) the ultimate goal for every believer in order to "walk in a manner worthy of the Lord, to please Him in all respects" (Colossians 1:10).

4a. Look at Ephesians 4:17-24. How does Paul describe unbelievers?

4b. As Christians we still struggle with the downward pull of the flesh referred to here as "your former manner of life." What should we do with "our old self?"

4c. What is the key to operating in "the new self?"

We all are assaulted with temptations from the world, the flesh, and the devil. These spiritual attacks are part of living in a fallen world. Learning to avoid these traps is the lifelong occupation for maturing Christians.

5. Read Romans 12:2. What must we do in order to live lives pleasing to the Lord?

Only when the mind is renewed by the Word of God can the life be (progressively) transformed. To this end, Paul prayed that we "may be filled with the knowledge of His will in all spiritual wisdom and understanding, so that [we] will walk in a manner worthy of the Lord, to please Him in all respects, bearing fruit in every good work and increasing in the knowledge of God" (Colossians 1:9-10).

FIXER UPPER

Everyone in the body of Christ has differing gifts and callings. 1 Corinthians 12:4-6 says, "Now there are varieties of gifts, but the same Spirit. And there are varieties of ministries, and the same Lord. There are varieties of effects but the same God who works all things in all persons." 1 Corinthians 12:18 says, "Now God has placed the members, each one of them, in the body, just as He desired." Obviously each of us has different functions within the body, but we are all called to be students of the Word of God.

Personal Bible study is to be intentional and systematic. Bible study is not to be restricted to an organized gathering to study the Word. Daily, read and meditate on the Word of God and spend time in prayer to aid in the process of renewing the mind and transforming the life.

Write out Romans 12:2 on an index card and put it in a place where you will see it several times a day. Throughout this week, memorize this vital scripture and meditate on its truth.

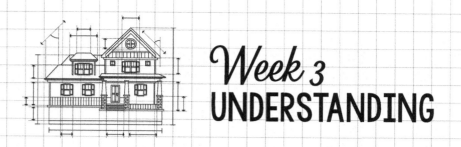

Week 3
UNDERSTANDING

DAY TWO

Today as we study the key word "understanding" we will be using a New Testament text as our backdrop. The account of the feeding of the 4000 is recorded in Mark 8:1-21. (An account of this miracle is also recorded in Matthew 15:32-39.) Only a short time before this event the disciples had been active participants in the feeding of 5000 which is mentioned in all four Gospels. This gathering in Mark 8 was primarily Jewish men, women, and children. It occurred on the northeast shore of Galilee near the town of Bethsaida.

Jesus remained in that area ministering to the people and teaching His disciples. In order to broaden their understanding of the reach of the gospel, Jesus brought the Twelve into the Gentile land surrounding Galilee. Mark 7:31 says, "He went out from the region of Tyre, and came through Sidon to the Sea of Galilee, within the region of Decapolis." Decapolis was comprised of ten cities that were under the rule of Syria. They had their own army, court system, and currency and they enjoyed a high level of Gentile culture. In this event when 4000 were fed, only the men were counted. The women and children were not counted, but were fed, so the number of those who experienced this miraculous meal could easily have been around 10,000 or even higher. This three-day event happened during a time of intense training for the disciples as Christ began in earnest to prepare them for His impending death. The cross was beginning to loom large and Jesus was teaching His disciples what His death, burial, and resurrection would mean for the Kingdom of God.

Jesus' ministry to the Gentiles was laying the groundwork for the Great Commission. Matthew 28:19 says, "Go therefore and make disciples of all the nations, baptizing them in the name of the Father and the Son and the Holy Spirit, teaching them to observe all that I commanded you; and lo, I am with you always, even to the end of the age." These Jewish disciples needed to understand that salvation is for the whole world, including the Gentiles. These men, raised in Israel, believed Gentiles were "excluded from the commonwealth of Israel, and strangers to the covenants of promise, having no hope and without God in the world" (Ephesians 2:12). In their minds, Gentiles were outside the salvation purpose of God and Israel alone was the nation God favored. Jesus had been ministering among the Gentiles to demonstrate the compassion of God and the invitation of salvation for the world. "There is no distinction between Greek and Jew, circumcised and uncircumcised, barbarian, Scythian, slave and freeman, but Christ is all, and in all" (Colossians 3:11). 1 John 2:2 says, "He Himself is the propitiation for our sins; and not for ours only, but also for those of the whole world." How would His disciples engage in the Great Commission and take the saving message of Christ to the world if they had not seen Jesus ministering to these people?

1a. Read Mark 8:1-9. Describe Jesus' concern for these people.

1b. What food was on hand according to the disciples?

1c. Jesus blessed the food and miraculously created something out of nothing. In doing so He surely was affirming His part in creation (see Genesis 1:31; John 1:3). The people "ate and were satisfied" (Mark 8:8). How much was leftover?

Try to imagine what the disciples were thinking. A Jew avoided any contact with Gentiles. They would never share a meal or even touch a Gentile. Yet, at the Lord's direction they are serving those considered outside the covenant blessings of Israel! Now, they are feeding Gentiles, ministering to them, and mingling with them, which violated everything they had been instructed from Judaism. Jesus was teaching the Twelve and demonstrating to the Gentiles that He had come to offer the Bread of Life to all humanity, both Jews and Gentiles. Staggering truth for His disciples to grasp!

After the multitudes were fed and satisfied, miraculously with seven loaves and "a few small fish" (Mark 8:7), the disciples "picked up seven large baskets full of what was left over of the broken pieces" (Mark 8:8). The grand finale culminated in the excess of leftovers underscoring the fact Jesus is capable of providing superabundantly. Ephesians 3:20-21 says, "Now to Him who is able to do far more abundantly beyond all that we ask or think, according to the power that works within us, to Him be the glory in the church and in Christ Jesus to all generations forever and ever. Amen."

Immediately Jesus "entered the boat with His disciples and came to the district of Dalmanutha" (Mark 8:10). On the heels of the miraculous feeding of the 4000, Jesus was confronted by religious leaders who did not believe He was the Messiah. "The Pharisees came out and began to argue with Him, seeking from Him a sign from heaven, to test Him" (Mark 8:11). The recent miraculous event when Jesus fed 4000 was not enough to convince them of His deity. Moses brought down bread from heaven and fed the children of Israel during their trek in the wilderness (see John 6:30-33). Jesus sighed "deeply in His spirit" (Mark 8:12) over the spiritually blind condition of these religious rulers who wanted "a sign from heaven" (Mark 8:11) before they would accept Him as Messiah. Possibly, Jesus felt no obligation to give a sign because ample opportunity had been given for those with eyes to see and ears to hear. His only response was to leave that region and go to Bethsaida. "Leaving them, He again embarked and went away to the other side" (Mark 8:13).

2. Read Mark 8:10-16. Jesus made a hasty exit and crossed over the Sea of Galilee to the other side. What did the disciples forget to take with them?

The lack of food was soon a topic of discussion among the disciples. The original language implies they were debating, possibly in order to assign blame to the guilty party. We can all relate to the disciples' reaction to skipping a meal! Jesus interrupted their bickering and warned them of "the leaven of the Pharisees and the leaven of Herod" (Mark 8:15). Leaven is generally used in the Bible to symbolize sin. Hypocrisy, spiritual pride, and legalism are "the leaven of the Pharisees." Jesus and His disciples had just witnessed this in their encounter with the Pharisees who took such pride in their religious rituals they failed to recognize their lost state. "The leaven of Herod" speaks of worldly compromise generally for the purpose of impressing others.

The disciples had just witnessed a miraculous event when 4000 (plus the women and children) had not just been fed, but "were satisfied" (Mark 8:8). They probably still had the crumbs of this supernatural bread in their beards and the smell of fish on their hands. Now, suddenly, they are worried about not having any bread to eat!

The baskets the disciples used to gather the leftovers were like hampers with handles common in the Gentile culture. Evidently they unloaded the baskets of bread before or during the encounter with the Pharisees. How could they have missed the large baskets of bread when they launched out? Had they become indifferent to the miracles Jesus was performing among the Jews and the Gentiles? Is it possible their racial bigotry against the Gentiles caused them to reject the bread tainted by the Gentile people in that region? The Bible does not give us any indication of the cause behind the missing bread, but we are staggered that the disciples ever let such miraculous provisions out of their sight. The inference of the disciples quickly forgetting God's good works should serve as a warning to us!

The disciples forgot to remember. Sadly, we are often stricken with the malady of forgetting the firsthand, marvelous and miraculous works of God in our lives.

3a. Look up 2 Peter 1:12-15. Let's pause in our study for a moment to consider a similar concern Peter had for his flock. What was Peter's concern?

3b. What was he willing to do in order to help them?

3c. In practical terms how can we avoid forgetting what we already know?

Now, back to our passage in Mark. The disciples participated in the feeding of the 5000 and the 4000. They were supposed to gain spiritual insight from these miracles confirming beyond a shadow of doubt that Jesus was the Messiah, the eternal Creator and Giver of Life. They were in the boat with the Son of God, but they could not trust Him to meet their physical needs as well as their spiritual ones. The divine irony of it all would be laughable if it weren't so sad and **so familiar**! How quickly we forget the faithfulness of our Lord and Savior Jesus Christ!

Psalm 34:8 says, "O taste and see that the Lord is good; how blessed is the man who takes refuge in Him!" We must have a regular intake of God's Word and become students of Scripture. His Word renews our minds, cleanses our hearts, softens our wills, and strengthens our spirits so that we become lost in His majesty!

4. Look once again at Mark 8:16. What did the disciples do right after Jesus' instructions to them cautioning them against the leaven of sin?

Jesus was astounded by their response. He was teaching them profound spiritual truth and yet they were focused on their missed meal!

5a. Read Mark 8:17-21. What was Jesus' reaction?

5b. What miracles did He reference?

In Mark 8:17-18 Jesus, seemingly indignant with the spiritual sluggishness of the disciples, asked, "Why do you discuss the fact that you have no bread? Do you not yet see or understand? Do you have a hardened heart? Having eyes, do you not see? And having ears, do you not hear? And do you not remember?" A lack of spiritual understanding indicated the disciples momentarily forgot who Jesus was and what He had miraculously done in the recent past. They also seemed to miss the spiritual lesson that Jesus was the Bread of Life for the whole world, including the Jews and the Gentiles.

The disciples had ample opportunities to see Jesus perform miracles. Beyond the feeding of the 5000 and the feeding of 4000, the disciples had front row seats and were eyewitnesses of a multitude of miracles, all pointing to the deity of Christ. John wrote, "Therefore many other signs Jesus also performed in the presence of the disciples, which are not written in this book; but these have been written so that you may believe that Jesus is the Christ, the Son of God; and that believing you may have life in His name" (John 20:30-31).

6. How can you guard your own heart to avoid becoming calloused and hardened to the miraculous wonder of Christ?

Jesus saw the same type of stubbornness characterizing the religious Pharisees and the Herodians as was evidenced by the Twelve. The unbelief of the disciples was bordering on that of Jesus' enemies. The disciples had heard Jesus teaching saying, "For this reason I say to you, do not be worried about your life, as to what you will eat or what you will drink; nor for your body, as to what you will put on. Is not life more than food, and the body more than clothing?" (Matthew 6:25). In Matthew 6:31-33 Jesus said, "Do not worry then, saying, 'What will we eat?' or 'What will we drink?' or 'What will we wear for clothing?' For the Gentiles eagerly seek all these things; for your heavenly Father knows that you need all these things. But seek first His kingdom and His righteousness, and all these things will be added to you." Yet, when faced with a difficulty, the disciples were looking through earthly eyes rather than spiritual ones, a trap we often fall into as well.

The disciples failed to "understand", which is our key word of this week's study. Their lack of understanding seemed to stem from their inability to discern the facts of their experience and reach a correct conclusion and gain a spiritual principle to govern their behavior. In other words, they were not able to take a practical lesson and gain spiritual insight.

The question for us remains, "Do you not yet see or understand? Do you have a hardened heart? Having eyes, do you not see? And having ears, do you not hear? And do you not remember? (Mark 8:17-18). "Do you not yet understand?" (Mark 8:21). As Christians, we too often suffer from a short memory concerning the things of God.

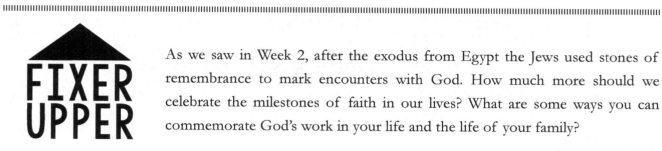

As we saw in Week 2, after the exodus from Egypt the Jews used stones of remembrance to mark encounters with God. How much more should we celebrate the milestones of faith in our lives? What are some ways you can commemorate God's work in your life and the life of your family?

Beloved, may we aggressively pursue lives of personal holiness and practical righteousness for the glory of Jesus Christ.

DAY THREE

Biblical understanding is the ability to assess a situation through the filter of the Word of God, ascertain God's purpose and direction, and apply His wisdom. The proper application of knowledge, understanding, and wisdom (progressively) produces a transformed life. A working knowledge of God's Word is necessary. A predetermined desire to walk in His ways is imperative. And courage to walk in God's wisdom is required. Psalm 1:1 says, "How blessed is the man who does not walk in the counsel of the wicked, nor stand in the path of sinners, nor sit in the seat of scoffers!" As Psalm 119:34 says, Lord Jesus, please "give [us] understanding, that [we] may observe Your law and keep it with all [our hearts]."

The blueprint for today's study is found in John 6:59-71. Please read this passage. I will give you a bit of background to shed more light on this event. Jesus has been teaching the Jewish people in the synagogue at Capernaum declaring Himself to be the Bread of Life.

> Therefore the Jews were grumbling about Him, because He said, 'I am the bread that came down out of heaven.' They were saying, 'Is not this Jesus, the son of Joseph, whose father and mother we know?' How does He now say, 'I have come down out of heaven'? (John 6:41-42).

Such a proclamation stunned the Jews! He followed up by saying, "I am the living bread that came down out of heaven; if anyone eats of this bread, he will live forever; and the bread also which I will give for the life of the world is My flesh" (John 6:51). This reference to the cross, as well as His assertion to being co-equal and co-eternal with the Father, reeked of blasphemy to the Jews. These references to eating His flesh and drinking His blood were merely a picture of the greater spiritual truth of a total surrender to Christ required in order to be saved. The Jews objected to His teaching. Jesus claimed to be the Bread of Life who came down from heaven. He taught He was God in human flesh and He was the only way to have eternal life. He spoke of His sacrifice and His blood. The Jews were becoming more and more infuriated by what He was teaching.

Great crowds were following Him but not all had committed themselves to Him by faith. These were people who had been drawn in through our Lord's teachings, which were often accompanied by miracles.

1. Look again at John 6:59-60. What was the reaction of the crowd in the synagogue where Jesus was teaching?

People were enamored with Jesus and excited about His ministry. It is interesting to note that it was not **the works** of Jesus (such as healing the blind and lame, delivering demon possessed people, feeding the multitudes, ministering to the poor, receiving the little children, and even raising the dead) that incensed the Jews; it was **the words** of Jesus. He taught about sin and the need of a Savior. He spoke of a personal surrender to Him, the shedding of His blood, and His sacrificial death. Jesus knew the audience was discontent with His teaching. In John 6:61 He asked, "Does this cause you to stumble?"

The Jews heard Jesus and they grumbled. They muttered. They murmured. They complained. Discontentment quickly spread throughout the crowd. I don't think we can pass up a chance to do a brief study of the power of the words we speak. Beloved, we must learn to guard our words! They are powerful and they have the potential to bring healing or hurt, blessings or bruises to the hearer.

2. Look up the following verses in 2 Timothy and write out the admonition to carefully select our words.

2 Timothy 2:14

2 Timothy 2:16-17

2 Timothy 2:23

We need to avoid unkind words. Proverbs 16:24 says, "Pleasant words are a honeycomb, sweet to the soul and healing to the bones." We need to avoid sarcasm. Proverbs 26:18-19 says, "Like a madman who throws firebrands, arrows, and death, so is the man who deceives his neighbor, and says, 'Was I not joking?'" Sarcasm is the use of irony to mock or convey contempt disguised with a thin veil of humor. We need to carefully choose our words and our tone. In Ephesians 4:29 Paul wrote, "Let no unwholesome word proceed from your mouth, but only such a word as is good for edification according to the need of the moment, so that it will give grace to those who hear." This is a powerful plumb line to measure our words. We need to speak the truth in love. Colossians 4:6, "Let your speech always be with grace, as though seasoned with salt, so that you will know how you should respond to each person." Make this your prayer, "Let the words of my mouth and the meditation of my heart be acceptable in Your sight, O Lord, my rock and my Redeemer" (Psalm 19:14).

Back to our text. Jesus knew there were those in the crowds following Him who did not truly believe. Many were merely enamored with Him but their heart condition was unchanged. The closer Jesus got to the cross, the more pointed His words became and the more offensive they were to the multitudes. Aware of the growing malice towards Him and His message, Jesus asked, "What then if you see the Son of Man ascending to where He was before?" (John 6:62). His question was parenthetical. The Lord knew the majority of the Jewish crowd had turned their allegiance away from Him and they would not be present to witness the death, burial, resurrection, or ascension.

Jesus said, "The words that I have spoken to you are spirit and are life" (John 6:63). Perhaps the final straw for many of the Jews in the crowd was when Jesus declared, "No one can come to Me unless it has been granted him from the Father" (John 6:65). Jesus' inclusion of Himself in the Trinity as the one and only way to God settled it for many in the crowd that day. They had rejected the Messiah and had sealed their fate for eternity. "As a result of this many of His disciples withdrew and were not walking with Him anymore. So Jesus said to the twelve, 'You do not want to go away also, do you?'" (John 6:66-67).

3. Look at John 6:68-69. What was Peter's response to Jesus' penetrating question?

The disciples' understanding of the Lord was disclosed to them by the Holy Spirit. Peter's confession of Christ for himself and the other disciples excluded Judas and stands in stark contrast to Judas' betrayal of Jesus Christ.

4. Look again at John 6:70-71. What did Jesus say concerning Judas?

The disciples, with the exception of Judas, had exercised genuine saving faith. Judas' deception did not take the Lord Jesus by surprise. Judas had been given the same opportunity as the other eleven men to act in repentance and faith, but he rejected and betrayed Jesus for thirty pieces of silver (see Matthews 26:14-17).

Beloved, do you know Jesus? Has there ever been a time in your life when you have repented of your sin and received Jesus? For more information on this topic please look in the Appendix for the resource entitled, "How to Become a Christian." If you are a part of this study and you do not know Jesus personally, He is calling to you and giving you an opportunity to be gloriously saved by grace through faith. Do not be among the multitude that heard, but responded in unbelief. The Bible promises, "Whoever will call on the name of the Lord will be saved" (Romans 10:13). We invite you to repent, believe, and receive Jesus today as your Lord and Savior.

As we have regular intake of the Word of God and desire to walk in the flow of the Holy Spirit, our understanding will be quickened by the Spirit of God. The Spirit enlightens us and enables us to walk in faith. Faith is characterized by our obedience to the Word of God, dependence on the Spirit of God, and confidence in the Son of God. Therefore, may the prayer of our hearts be, " Teach [us], O Lord, the way of Your statutes, and [we] shall observe it to the end. Give [us] understanding, that [we] may observe Your law and keep it with all [our] heart" (Psalm 119:33-34). Amen and amen!

Week 3
UNDERSTANDING

DAY FOUR

The word "understanding" has been our key word this week. In order to have Biblical understanding, we must apply ourselves as students of the Word and rely on the Holy Spirit to enlighten us. In doing so we will hammer out personal convictions to serve as parameters in our lives to the glory of God.

The Lord often taught in parables. He frequently used an earthly illustration in order to teach a greater spiritual truth. In Matthew 13:10-11 says, "And the disciples came and said to Him, 'Why do You speak to them in parables?' Jesus answered them, 'To you it has been granted to know the mysteries of the kingdom of heaven, but to them it has not been granted.'" Large crowds were following Him, enamored by His speaking prowess which was often accompanied by miracles. Jesus, discerning the condition of those who flocked to hear Him, knew that many had not experienced a heart change. They did not believe in Him. They had eyes to see but were blind to spiritual truth. They had ears but were dull of hearing. They could not understand because they did not want to know the truth. Therefore Jesus spoke in parables to spiritually veil His teaching from those who had outright rejected Him in their hearts. But to His disciples He said, "Blessed are your eyes, because they see; and your ears, because they hear" (Matthew 13:16).

1a. Read Matthew 13:24-30. Jesus was speaking a parable of the tares and the wheat to expound on the kingdom of heaven. To what can the kingdom of heaven be compared? A landowner "sowed good seed in his field." Typically he and his crew would have plowed the soil, cleared out the rocks and weed, and carefully prepared the soil to receive the seeds in favor of a good harvest. While his crew was sleeping after a long hard day of sowing seed "his enemy came."

1b. The nefarious deed was not immediately noticed. When "the wheat sprouted and bore grain," what became evident?

Sowing tares in a wheat field had the potential of ruining a landowner. This practice of sowing weeds among freshly planted fields was so widespread the Roman government passed a law against it.

Evidently, the wheat plants and the tares look identical in the immature stage. The difference becomes visible when the head of grain appears on the wheat stalk. When the servants saw the fields full of weed they approached the landowner and asked if they should gather the tares.

2. What reply did the master give? (vv. 29-30)

We read Jesus' explanation of the parable of the wheat and tares in Matthew 13:36-43. Read this passage and answer the following questions.

3a. Who is the Sower?

What does the field represent?

What does the good seed represent?

Who are the tares?

3b. Jesus identifies the enemy. Who is he?

3c. What does the harvest represent?

3d. Who are the reapers in this parable?

God reveals His truth to believers and grants them understanding through His Word and His Spirit. Just a reminder. Prior to the Day of Pentecost when the Holy Spirit came to inhabit individual believers, the disciples and others who believed did not have the indwelling Holy Spirit. The only Bible they had was the Old Testament. Therefore, Jesus was careful to explain truth to them to help them understand. We have the indwelling Holy Spirit and the full revelation of God in the Old and New Testament. Therefore, His Word serves as our "external" guide and His Spirit serves as our "internal" guide to enlighten our understanding. For the unbeliever, this is not so. 1 Corinthians 1:18 says, "For the word of the cross is foolishness to those who are perishing, but to us who are being saved it is the power of God." 1 Corinthians 2:14 says, "A natural man does not accept the things of the Spirit of God, for they are foolishness to him; and he cannot understand them, because they are spiritually appraised."

Tares and wheat. Unbelievers and believers growing together. God has planted us as it pleased Him throughout the world, knowing we would live among those who do not believe. Jesus said, "Behold, I send you out as sheep in the midst of wolves; so be shrewd as serpents and innocent as doves" (Matthew 10:16). We are to be wise as serpents and gentle as doves as we navigate living in a fallen world. John 16:33 says, "In the world you have tribulation, but take courage; I have overcome the world."

At the end of the age "The Son of Man will send forth His angels, and they will gather out of His kingdom all stumbling blocks, and those who commit lawlessness, and will throw them into the furnace of fire; in that place there will be weeping and gnashing of teeth" (Matthew 13:41-42). Eternal damnation awaits those who reject Christ. Hell will be a place of torment and inescapable judgment separated from Jesus Christ and His people. We are not called to identify the tares for judgment. That is God's responsibility. He is the ultimate judge. For now, God will permit the righteous and the wicked "to grow together until the harvest" (Matthew 13:30). At "the end of the age" (Matthew 13:39) He will separate the wicked, judge them, and cast them into the lake of fire (see Revelation 20:11-15) while gathering the righteous together to be rewarded and to enjoy His presence for all eternity.

What are we to do? How then shall we live? The role of believers is to share Christ with the unbelieving world. Prior to our conversion we were tares in the wheat field. Someone shared the Gospel with us and we responded to the Lord's invitation to receive the free gift of salvation with repentance and faith. "For by grace you have been saved through faith; and that not of yourselves, it is the gift of God; not as a result of works, so that no one may boast" (Ephesians 2:8-9). We are to be intentional as a Bible student, a prayer warrior, and a soul winner in order to advance the Kingdom of God. "The Lord's bond-servant must not be quarrelsome, but be kind to all, able to teach, patient when wronged, with gentleness correcting those who are in opposition, if perhaps God may grant them repentance leading to the knowledge of the truth, and they may come to their senses and escape from the snare of the devil, having been held captive by him to do his will" (2 Timothy 2:24-26).

4. Look up Philippians 2:14-16. According to this passage what are we called to be?

We live in a broken, crooked world. May we be ambassadors for Christ, saturated with the aroma of Jesus, sharing the gospel, and serving the Kingdom of God until He comes!

DAY FIVE

I trust we have built a solid foundation concerning our key word "understanding." In the biblical sense, "understanding" is gained through the study of God's Word and the illumination of the Spirit of God.

2 Peter 1:2-3 says, "Grace and peace be multiplied to you in the knowledge of God and of Jesus our Lord; seeing that His divine power has granted to us everything pertaining to life and godliness, through the true knowledge of Him who called us by His own glory and excellence." God has given us everything we need to live for His glory through His Word and His Spirit. The Word of God is alive. "For the word of God is living and active and sharper than any two-edged sword, and piercing as far as the division of soul and spirit, of both joints and marrow, and able to judge the thoughts and intentions of the heart" (Hebrews 4:12). The Spirit of God is alive in us.

Romans 8:16-17 says, "The Spirit Himself testifies with our spirit that we are children of God, and if children, heirs also, heirs of God and fellow heirs with Christ." When the living Word of God and the Spirit of God come together in our lives, the power of God is released. However, while these supernatural resources **are available** to all believers, an enlightened understanding and the ability to access them **are not automatic**. Intentional and systematic study of the Word of God in conjunction with a surrendered will to the promptings of the Holy Spirit is a necessity!

The moment in time of our conversion is often referred to as regeneration. Regeneration is followed by a process called sanctification. This is the progressive transformation of being changed into the image of Christ. "We all, with unveiled face, beholding as in a mirror the glory of the Lord, are being transformed into the same image from glory to glory, just as from the Lord, the Spirit" (2 Corinthians 3:18). Sanctification is often slow and sometimes painful. The cornerstone of sanctification, out of necessity, has to be obedience to the Lord. Obedience is the basic mark of genuine conversion and should be increasingly evident as we grow in the grace and knowledge of the Lord. Please do not misunderstand me. I am writing about the process of spiritual maturity. I am not referring to striving to achieve perfection; it is not even a realistic goal. We will not be perfect until we see Jesus. While locked in these earthly vessels, we are going to sin. The downward pull of the world, the flesh, and the devil will continually tempt us and at times, we will fall into sin.

The beloved apostle Paul wrote about his battle with sin (probably he is referencing his experience as a new believer in Christ) in Romans 7:15, "For what I am doing, I do not understand; for I am not practicing what I would like to do, but I am doing the very thing I hate." We will continue to sin after our conversion, but our desire and goal as daughters of the King should be to avoid sin at all costs. Proverbs 24:16 says, "For a righteous man falls seven times, and rises again." The more spiritually mature we become the less we sin and the more we hate it when we do. John wrote, "By this we know that we have come to know Him, if we keep His commandments" (1 John 2:3). A renewed mind resulting in a transformed life will be evident and serve to validate our genuine conversion.

Read James 1:22-25.

James likens the Word of God to a mirror. In this text, James contrasts those who are merely hearers of the Word with those who obey the Word. Commentators are divided on the issue if the hearer of the Word is an unbeliever or a Christian. Since the illustration can suggest either distinction, for our purposes we will refer to them as casual Christians without doing any damage to the text.

1a. How does James describe hearers of the Word?

1b. How does James describe doers of the Word?

Mirrors in the first century were not made of glass. They were made of metal and had to be polished regularly in order to avoid tarnishing. Mirrors rested horizontally on tables so a person had to bend over and look down. By looking in a mirror, one can observe his outward appearance and identify areas that need attention. James uses this analogy to illustrate that those who hear the Word without acting in obedience to it are like the man who looks at his natural face in a mirror and immediately forgets what he saw. This could be likened to the casual believer who attended a worship service or Bible study, heard the Word of God proclaimed, and "immediately forgot what kind of person he was" (James 1:24). He heard the Word, but failed to respond to its demands and walked away unchanged. Those in this category "delude themselves" (James 1:22). Sadly, the exposure to the Word of God without application or obedience leads to being self-deceived. Such a man thinks he has bettered himself spiritually when he has actually harmed himself.

The casual glance of a hearer of the Word is in sharp contrast to the person who bends over to look "intently at the perfect law, the law of liberty, and abides by it, not having become a forgetful hearer but an effectual doer" (James 1:25). As we look intently at the Word of God, it reveals our heart and points out sin. The Spirit of God enables us to deal with it through repentance and confession.

2a. Read 1 John 1:9. This sweet promise is conditional. What is required from us?

2b. What will God do when we deal with sin according to His Word?

In order to gain understanding there must be a willing cooperation on our part to God's revelation, whether written or spoken. Obedience is required if the Word is to actively transform us. The doer of the Word of God is aggressively pursuing personal holiness and practical righteousness which result in a transformed life.

James attaches a blessing to those who study God's Word with a view to putting it into practice. "An effectual doer . . . will be blessed in what he does" (James 1:25). A life of fulfillment, outrageous joy, peace that cannot be put into words, and overwhelming love is only possible through a personal relationship with Christ and a determination to understand His Word and walk in His ways.

Psalm 19:7-8 says, "The law of the Lord is perfect, restoring the soul; the testimony of the Lord is sure, making wise the simple. The precepts of the Lord are right, rejoicing the heart; the commandment of the Lord is pure, enlightening the eyes." Determine to never be a forgetful hearer of the Word. Make the study of God's Word a priority as an effectual doer of the Word. Be blessed, beloved!

Week 4
KNOWLEDGE

The fear of the Lord is the beginning of knowledge.
Proverbs 1:7a

In the lessons for the last two weeks, we have contemplated the concepts of both wisdom and understanding. We learned that a house is built by wisdom and established by understanding. This week we will reflect on knowledge. In Proverbs 24:4, we read "by knowledge the rooms are filled with every precious and beautiful treasure"(HCSB). Let's delve right into the meaning of knowledge this week and discover the blueprint for a home filled with the knowledge of God.

In the early years of our marriage, my husband and I bought a piece of property on which to build a house. I remember our excitement as we met with the architect to conceptualize the plans. We had honeymooned in historic Williamsburg and were enamored with the colonial architecture. We carefully considered the space we desired. The day came when the blueprints were ready and we reviewed them with great anticipation. Yet a funny thing happened on the way to build our new house—we got a great buy on a fixer-upper! And a fixer-upper it was—pink cabinets and gray floors in the kitchen, gray and pink wallpaper in the master bedroom, carpet covering the hardwood floors, and much, much more. It definitely wasn't a current look of that time period. And unfortunately, there was no HGTV around at the time.

While I am writing this study, workmen are installing new siding on various places on my fixer-upper. Yes, we still live there. Actually, it has gone through several renovations throughout the years. I've been sitting on pins and needles hoping that the contractor would not contact me with the problem that inevitably comes up on the fixer-upper shows—so far, so good. Frankly, these problems typically come as surprises because of a lack of knowledge, a topic we will spend a lot of time on this week. Knowledge is crucial when you are building your house of faith.

DAY ONE

The quest for knowledge is as old as time itself beginning in The Garden. Philosophers through the ages have discussed its intricacies in the discipline called epistemology. Mankind has always searched for knowledge and truth.

1. Using a dictionary, write a secular definition of knowledge.

The Merriam-Webster Dictionary gives this definition of knowledge:

- The fact or condition of knowing something with familiarity gained through experience or association

- Acquaintance with understanding of a science, art, or technique

- The sum of what is known: the body of truth, information, and principles acquired by humankind[24]

The secular definition of knowledge encompasses knowledge acquired by experience or education. However, in order to understand our text, we need to look deeper to discover the meaning of the knowledge to which the author of Proverbs is referring. In the original Hebrew, the word used for knowledge is *da'at* meaning: to know, knowledge, insight, intelligence, understanding, wisdom, cunning. Though it is a general term for knowledge, it can also be personal.

2. According to Proverbs 2:4-6, what kind of knowledge should we seek? Where does this knowledge come from?

3. Read the following verses to discover where knowledge begins.

Proverbs 1:7

Proverbs 9:10

Psalm 111:10

4. From your perspective, what does it mean to fear the Lord?

In the original Hebrew language, the word *Yir'ah* translated as fear is defined as: fear, terror, reverence, awe, piety. It can denote a reverence for the Lord as it does in the verses we read in question three. This excerpt from the *Women's Evangelical Commentary on the Old Testament* provides a very thought-provoking explanation of the fear of the Lord.

> You cannot "fear the Lord" without first giving up your own desires and turning from your own way. In so doing you willingly accept God's rebuke and correction and accept His mandates, which in turn lead to personal piety and a life set apart unto Him. This concept is synonymous with intimate knowledge of God and understanding of His ways. It cannot be separated from an understanding of the holiness of God.
>
> To fear the Lord is to move beyond a reverential trust in Him. Rather you know that the Lord is not only watching what you do; He is also listening to what you say, and He is reading your thoughts before they are verbalized. You are constantly aware that you are in the presence of the holy, just, all-powerful God of the universe. You realize that every thought in your mind, every word from your mouth, every action in your life—all are open before Him and thus will be judged by Him. There is a controlling awe emanating from an understanding of His power and righteous retribution as well as the bonds of a deep-seated love that prompts in your heart a wholesome dread of doing anything to displease Him, whom you love more than life itself.[25]

5. My friend, does this passage describe you? Is your day-to-day life characterized by a reverent fear of the Lord? Do you know Him and His Word so intimately that you can say you walk in knowledge? Take a moment to reflect on this and write your thoughts.

6. Read Proverbs 31:30. What does God value in a woman? How does it compare to what the world frequently values?

As we considered our quest for knowledge today, we learned in the first chapter of Proverbs that the fear of the Lord is the beginning of knowledge and in the final chapter, we noted the great value that God places on the woman who fears him. Obviously, this reverential fear and awe is a very important part of our walk with the Lord. Let's consciously consider our great and awesome God and let the knowledge of Who He is transform us.

As you reflect on what it means to apply the Biblical concept of the fear of the Lord to your daily life, ponder this quote from Sung Wook Chung and seek to make personal application to your life.

> We should strive to know God. Unless we gain a true knowledge of God, we can't fear him in an appropriate manner. In order to know God, we should focus on what he has revealed about himself. Since God reveals himself in the Scripture, we should read, study, and meditate on the Word of God in order to know about God. Of course, this informational "head" knowledge about God needs to be accompanied by a "heart" knowledge and personal experience of God. This experience takes place through our personal worship of God and a personal life of prayer, obedience, and witness. Therefore, we should do our best to worship God in the truth and the Spirit, to pray to God earnestly, to obey God's Word, and to witness faithfully to the grace of God in Jesus Christ.[26]

Week 4
KNOWLEDGE

DAY TWO

At the dawn of time, God spoke and, within the span of six days, created this majestic universe along with man and woman, Adam and Eve. God placed them in a garden filled with beauty and sustenance—providing absolutely everything they needed. Because God was desirous of a relationship with mankind, He would fellowship with them in the garden. Can you even imagine! I find it difficult to fathom a love so great that the Creator God in His omniscience, knowing the cost of mankind's disobedience, created us anyway. And yet He did. God only placed one restriction on garden life—do not eat of the tree of the knowledge of good and evil. God instructed Adam about this prohibition and he passed it on to Eve. So, Adam and Eve lived in their idyllic environment until one day they had a visitor—an adversary, an enemy, Satan. Having been cast out of heaven for rebellion against God, Satan's desire was to be like God. As he crawled into the garden disguised as a serpent, his intent was to plant that same desire in the mind of Eve.

1. Read Genesis 3:1-6. What specific elements were included in Satan's temptation of Eve?

2. How did Eve respond to Satan?

3. Describe Eve's reasoning and her decision.

4. As you read Genesis 3:8-24, record the results (immediate, long-term, physical and spiritual) of Adam's and Eve's decision.

5. How did the sin of Adam and Eve affect mankind? Do our sins impact others? If so, how?

All wisdom, knowledge and truth is from God. The enemy was very crafty to tempt Eve in the sphere of knowledge by telling her that her eyes would be opened and she would be like God. In the *Women's Evangelical Commentary Old Testament,* this explanation is given concerning Satan's lie:

> The phrase "your eyes will be opened" expresses a Hebrew metaphor for knowledge. "The serpent" intimated the value of what they would gain without mentioning what they would lose. He presented a curse as a blessing. Of course, if they had continued in obedience, their knowledge would have come from their fellowship with God. On the other hand, disobedience of the divine mandate would add a painful dimension to their understanding—learning the tragic and costly consequences to disobedience by experience. Truly they had received knowledge, the knowledge of what is good and what is evil, the knowledge of the consequences of sin and disobedience.[27]

Like Adam and Eve, we have an enemy. He is a real adversary—not a character dressed in a red suit carrying a pitchfork. We learn about him in the pages of Scripture so let's delve in to remind ourselves about some of the specifics of his character.

6. Investigate what Jesus had to say about the devil in John 8:44 and record what you find. Check out the verse in the NIV translation for an interesting insight.

7. Read the following verses and relate the characteristics of the devil found in them. Include any instructions you find for resisting his attacks.

1 Peter 5:8-9

2 Corinthians 11:14

James 4:7

Ephesians 6:10-18

Christopher Morton gives some practical instruction when considering Satan:

> Because Jesus took Satan very seriously, we are wise to do the same. Jesus understood Satan to be a real, personal, and intentional being who strives to oppose the will of God. At the same time, Jesus didn't inordinately focus on Satan, and we shouldn't either. While respecting the power of Satan and being aware of his ability to deceive us and lead us astray, we shouldn't give him the attention that only God deserves. To be aware of his wicked work, we can glance at Satan while we gaze at God. God alone deserves our focus. As the source of truth and goodness, he alone enables us to discern the devices of Satan as he works his deceptions.[28]

Satan is still using his strategy of whispering lies into our minds just as he did with Eve. Our challenge is to identify the lies and replace them with truth. God's Word is the repository of truth and the filter through which we evaluate every thought, action, and motive. When confronted with temptation, we must remember the downward spiral that it offers. James 1:13-15 reminds us of the danger:

> When tempted, no one should say, "God is tempting me." For God cannot be tempted by evil, nor does he tempt anyone; but each one is tempted when, by his own evil desire, he is dragged away and enticed. Then, after desire has conceived, it gives birth to sin; and sin, when it is full-grown, gives birth to death (NIV).

8. List the incremental steps leading from temptation to death.

9. Think about a time when you succumbed to temptation and consequently sinned. What was the precipitating factor—believing a lie or ignorance of the truth? What life lesson can you learn from the experience?

Tomorrow we will contemplate truth and how to discover it. Until then…

FIXER UPPER

Years ago, I read *The Search for Significance* by Robert McGee. In the book, Dr. McGee presented a very practical method to replace the lies of Satan with the truth of God's Word.

Dr. McGee maintains:

> A person's mind contains deeply held beliefs and attitudes which have been learned through environment, experiences, and education. These beliefs and attitudes produce thoughts which reflect how we perceive the events in our lives. These thoughts, then, are the foundations of our emotions, and emotions are the launching pad for actions.
>
> Many of our thoughts can be traced back to our beliefs—beliefs which are either founded on the truths of Scripture, or the lies of Satan.[29]

It is crucial to be able to identify the lies of the enemy. The key is to know God's Truth through a consistent study of the Bible. Then you will be able to identify the lies when they come your way.

DAY THREE

Yesterday we investigated the temptation of Adam and Eve in the garden which led to the eventual fall of mankind. As we contemplated the Scripture, we were reminded that we have a very real enemy, Satan, who is the father of lies—there is no truth in him. Satan and the world system bombards us with lies which makes it all the more important to have a knowledge of the truth. Mankind has been asking this question since time began, "What is truth?"

A simple definition would include that which is factual and not falsehood. Though that definition would stand in the light of Scripture, generally the meaning is far richer as illustrated in this definition in the *Hebrew-Greek Key Word Study Bible*.

Aletheia—Theologically, absolute truth, ultimate truth, transcendent truth, divinely revealed truth, true truth. Truth here refers to the reality of things in their relation to God.

1. In light of the definition above, read these verses and record the Psalmist's insight into truth.

    Psalm 25:4-5

    Psalm 51:6

    Psalm 86:11

    Psalm 119:160

The Psalmists recognized that truth comes from God, but it can be known by man as God reveals it. Dr. Adrian Rogers, the former pastor of Bellevue Baptist Church, used to quip, "Did it ever occur to you that nothing ever occurs to God?" God is now and always has been the author and source of truth.

However, we live in a world today where some people believe that there is no such thing as absolute truth or, for that matter, a God. What defines how you think about yourself and the world is known as worldview. Here is an explanation by Ergun Caner:

> In the most general terms, a worldview is the framework of beliefs by which a person views the world around him. In common parlance, it is the grid or filter through which a person interprets everything. For the Christian, that grid is the Bible. Scripture is the grid through which believers view existence, truth, sin, salvation, ethics, and evil.[30]

Each individual has a method through which he arrives at his worldview. Often it is entirely subjective based merely on feelings—whatever makes him happy or is compatible to his way of thinking. In this instance, two people might have a worldview in direct contradiction to one another as each one bases his worldview strictly on his subjective feelings. Perhaps this is the origination of the comment, "It might be true for you, but it is not true for me." Another method for determining worldview is based on society or culture. But, culture and laws change and the worldview collapses.

The biblical worldview holds that truth resides in the words of Scripture. Yet some will argue that other religions and cultures have viable worldviews which should be considered. The validity of the Bible has been confirmed by fulfilled prophecies, evidence from nonbiblical sources, and other verifications to provide confidence that it is the repository of truth needed to develop an authentic worldview. No other religion can truthfully claim the same. One's destiny is wrapped up in his worldview. Gregory Thornbury says it well: "A person's worldview is a roadmap to his soul: it shows where he will begin and where he will end up."[31]

2. What does the Apostle Paul proclaim about Jesus in Colossians 2:3? How could this knowledge change your life?

3. As John begins the narrative of his gospel, what does he relate concerning Jesus in John 1:14 and 17?

4. What does Jesus share about truth in these verses?

   John 14:6

   John 8:31-32

5. Explain the role of the Holy Spirit based on the following verses.

   John 14:16-17

   John 15:26

   John 16:13-14

I remember the big debate surrounding abortion before it was legalized in the United States in 1973. The topic saturated the newscasts with women demanding their rights, and was the subject of conversations throughout the country. Some of the arguments sounded persuasive when presented outside the parameters of Scripture. Though many in the culture were clamoring for this right, I knew without a doubt that it conflicted with the truth found in God's Word. The culture throws us one conundrum after another. How will we make our decisions? God's Truth will be our guide.

As we close our lesson on truth, let's concentrate on a few thought provoking questions:

6. Are you influenced by cultural thought? If so, in what area?

7. Does what you know about God's Word determine how you live day-in and day-out?

8. Name one of God's truths that has been distorted by a cultural worldview.

This is good, and it is pleasing in the sight of God our Savior, who desires
all people to be saved and to come to the knowledge of the truth.

1 Timothy 2:3-4 (ESV)

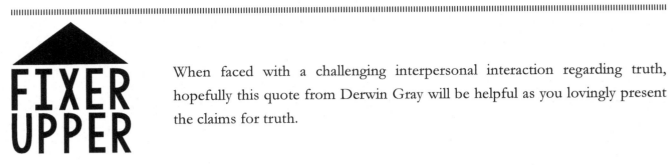

FIXER UPPER

When faced with a challenging interpersonal interaction regarding truth, hopefully this quote from Derwin Gray will be helpful as you lovingly present the claims for truth.

Jesus claimed that He was "the truth"—He did not claim to be one truth amongst many. The implications of this controversial and exclusive statement are eternal. We live in a postmodern culture that cringes at the thought of absolute truth. As evangelicals share Jesus as the exclusive path to God, and proclaim that it is His truth alone that reveals God to man, they will be bombarded with statements such as, "There is no truth," or "Truth is relative." How are evangelicals to respond to such post-modern responses?

When someone says, "There is no truth," ask that person, "Is that statement true?" When a person states there is no truth, he is making an absolute truth statement. When a person says, "Truth is relative," ask "Is that statement true or relative?" To say truth is relative is to make an absolute truth claim.[31]

In asking these simple questions, perhaps the other person will recognize that his statement is unsustainable. May this open up a genuine dialogue on truth.

DAY FOUR

We live in a world where counterfeits proliferate—money, cell phones, designer handbags and jewelry and the list could go on and on. Once my attorney husband had a client who was charged with selling counterfeit Rolex watches at the flea market. When the client faced the judge, he was ordered to discontinue selling the watches or face jail time. Since he had additional inventory on hand, he gave my husband a few of the watches. With Christmas fast approaching, we decided to play a joke on my brother. I wrapped a watch up beautifully in a Rolex watch box and put it under the tree. You should have seen the incredulous expression on my brother's face as he opened the box because at first glance, it looked so genuine. However, on closer scrutiny, he could tell that it did not measure up to an authentic Rolex watch. We had a good laugh but he did not add that counterfeit to his dress for success wardrobe.

The story goes that when an expert in identifying counterfeit money was asked how he did it successfully, he responded that he learned not by studying the counterfeit bills but rather by examining the originals. In our search for knowledge and truth, sometimes we will encounter counterfeit teaching and doctrine. Therefore, it is critical that we know God's Word in order to identify any teaching that does not measure up to God's authentic truth. Let's do exactly that today by investigating who Jesus is and what He has done for those of us who have trusted Him as our Savior. But first, I would like to share a quote from the *Women's Evangelical Commentary on the New Testament* which sheds some light on our assignment.

> Attacks of false teaching usually focus on two major issues: (1) the person of Jesus Christ and (2) the Christian's identity in Him. False teachers may deny that Jesus Christ is God, or they may undermine His personhood as being fully human. They often propose "something more" as necessary for the completion of salvation. Quasi-Christian cults have an easily identifiable "mathematical" formula: They subtract from the person of Jesus Christ and add to the method of salvation.[32]

The church has frequently had to contend with false doctrine—whether it was in the early church or in 1517 when Martin Luther led in the Reformation. Remember, we have an enemy who propagates lies seeking to lead the church astray. The Apostle Paul dealt with this issue in many of his epistles to the early churches. While there are many passages that address this problem, today we will look at Colossians and 2 Timothy. Like the currency expert who studies the original, in Colossians, Paul addresses the false teaching by pointing out what genuine faith in Jesus Christ looks like.

1. What admonition does the Apostle Paul give the Church at Colossae in Colossians 2:8?

2. Read these passages concerning the character of Jesus and what He has done for Christians and record your findings on the chart in the appropriate place.

   Colossians 1:11-20

   Colossians 2:9-15

The Character of Jesus	The Work of Jesus

Paul painted the portrait of the original and gave them an opportunity for comparison with the false doctrine. In essence, he was saying Jesus is God and He is enough—nothing else was needed.

In 2 Timothy, Paul speaks to the church of Ephesus regarding the last days—throughout church history, believers have thought that they lived in the last days. Certainly, our times would bring us to arrive at the same conclusion.

3a. Describe the people that Paul depicts from the last days in these passages.

   2 Timothy 3:1-5

   2 Timothy 4:3-4

3b. How are Christians to respond to these people?

4. Read 2 Timothy 3:6-7. What warning does Paul give concerning women in these verses?

Are you discerning and alert regarding false teaching? This quote from the *Women's Evangelical Commentary on the New Testament* is very thought provoking:

> Are you a gullible woman of the world or a godly woman of the Word? Many Christian women today have been led astray by the culture, following its practices and lifestyles. Paul gave a very convicting description of gullible women of the world in 2 Timothy 3:6-9. Gullible women are "burdened down with sins," "led along by a variety of passions," "always learning and never able to come to a knowledge of truth." The Bible is clear: Christians are to resist these false teachings and "flee" from immorality (2 Timothy 2:22-23).
>
> In contrast, Paul challenged believers to be godly women of the Word. Godly women follow true doctrine, live Christlike lives, seek God's purposes, grow in faith, develop patience, extend love and persevere in persecution. Christians are to live godly lives, remaining set apart from the world.[33]

When I was a child, my family knew a lovely, elderly woman, who was like another grandmother to me. She was drawn in by the false teaching of a cult and left her church in a mainstream Protestant denomination. Year after year, she diligently followed the ideology of that false religion. I have often wondered how she could have been so misled. It is critical that we can identify false teaching, so study what other religions believe—but much more importantly, be competent in Bible doctrine.

Be alert. Seek the truth in the Word. And do not neglect to speak the truth.

When Paul corresponded with the churches through his epistles, he challenged the believers to avoid counterfeit teaching. In the last few moments of our study today, reflect on the encouragement Paul sent Timothy, his son in the faith. May all of us take these words to heart and apply them to our lives.

> But as for you, continue in what you have learned and have firmly believed, knowing from whom you learned it and how from childhood you have been acquainted with the sacred writings, which are able to make you wise for salvation through faith in Christ Jesus (2 Timothy 3:14-15, ESV).

> O Timothy, guard the deposit entrusted to you. Avoid the irreverent babble and contradictions of what is falsely called "knowledge," for by professing it some have swerved from the faith. Grace be with you (1 Timothy 6:20-21, ESV).

DAY FIVE

Since I live in an older neighborhood, it has become quite routine for newly acquired houses to undergo an extensive renovation. Occasionally, a home will be purchased only to be entirely demolished and another home built on the site. I enjoy watching the process as I drive or walk through the neighborhood. When framework goes up, I can safely assume that they are adding on. Frequently, most of the work is transpiring on the inside and unseen from the outside. A glance at the dumpster, however, assures me that much is happening inside. I love observing the finished product. Recently, a renovation was completed and the results were so stunning that I found myself musing, "I could see myself living there." What was the appeal? It was inviting, restful, and beautiful—a place where I could feel at home.

As we consider our own spiritual homes, it might come to our attention that we might require a little renovation of our own. After watching the fixer-upper shows on HGTV, we know that it generally begins with some demolition. All the guys on those shows seem to love demo day, but truthfully, demo is hard work. Sometimes you discover problems below the surface that are costly and difficult to repair. But, in the end, the repairs are necessary and worth all the effort.

Yesterday, we walked through the first two chapters of Colossians with the Apostle Paul. He painted a glorious portrait of the Lord Jesus and His work on our behalf. He warned the church about false teachers and encouraged them to grow in their knowledge of God. Today, let's consider Colossians 3 where we can glean some practical knowledge concerning our spiritual growth.

1. Read Colossians 3:1-4. As Christians, where should our attention be focused? Why?

Now Paul begins to describe the process of demolition and renovation in the Christian's life. He reminds them of what they were before Christ and what qualities need to permeate their lives after salvation.

2. Read Colossians 3:5-14. Why should the believers take on this process of demolition and renovation? (v. 10)

Renovation begins with taking out the old and replacing it with the new. One of my favorite parts on the fixer-upper shows is watching the old, worn out, and dated fixtures being replaced with those which are new, fresh, and up to date. That was exactly what Paul was stressing to the believers in Colossae. They were new creations—so act like it.

3. On the chart, list the qualities that the believers were to demolish from their lives and the ones they were to add in order to live like newly renovated creations. (vs. 5-14)

Demolition	Renovation

4. What advice does Paul give the believers in Colossians 3:16?

In 2 Peter 1, we observe that Peter and Paul are in complete agreement concerning the necessity of the Christian's transformation. As new creations, they were to look different from the world.

5. Examine 2 Peter 1:1-4. What encouragement does Peter give the believers in their quest to live transformed lives? What is the source for a life of godliness?

Warren Wiersbe comments on the concept of renovation in the life of the believer:

> Where there is life, there must be growth. The new birth is not the end; it is the beginning. God gives His children all that they need to live godly lives, but His children must apply themselves and be diligent to use the "means of grace" He has provided. Spiritual growth is not automatic. It requires cooperation with God and the application of spiritual diligence and discipline.[34]

> You can usually tell when Christians are not growing, for they have these three characteristics: (1) They are barren, or idle; that is, they will not work for Christ. (2) They are unfruitful; that is, their meager knowledge of Christ does not produce fruit in their lives. (3) They are blind, lacking spiritual insight, spiritually "near-sighted." Behind this lack of spiritual development is a poor memory, forgetting what God has done for them through Christ.[35]

Peter continues in Chapter 1 to list qualities that should be evident in a believer's life beginning with faith and expanding to create a depiction of the mature Christian.

6. After reading 2 Peter 1:5-9, record the virtues mentioned. What does Peter share concerning those who lack them? Are these virtues apparent in your life?

Peter and Paul have challenged us on to maturity. We have learned what we need to demolish and what needs to be added. This reminds me of my favorite part of the fixer upper shows—the reveal of the finished product. The flashbacks prompt recollections of what the house looked like previously. Then we see the fruit of the renovation. The contrast is astounding. The old has been removed and the new is revealed—new fixtures, new furniture, new accessories, sometimes even a new floor plan—a total transformation.

I perceive a striking correlation between the houses that have been renovated and the house that the writer of Proverbs refers to. They are houses where people want to live—inviting, restful, beautiful. Remember our text for this study from Proverbs 24:3-4:

> By wisdom a house is built, and by understanding it is established; and by knowledge the rooms are filled with all precious and pleasant riches.

On TV the houses are filled with beautiful furniture and accessories. What are the riches that should fill our houses? I believe they are outlined for us by Paul and Peter. Paul suggested compassion, kindness, humility, gentleness, patience, forbearance, forgiveness, and love. Peter mentioned moral excellence, knowledge, self-control, perseverance, godliness, brotherly kindness, and love. Note that both Paul and Peter ended with love. Imagine a house filled with all these qualities and tied up with love! I want to live there. Don't you?

Our passage informs us that the rooms are filled by knowledge, making our quest for knowledge of utmost importance. The knowledge referred to here is not just information, but rather what we find from a consistent study of God's Word and what it reveals about Jesus Christ, what He has done on our behalf, who we are in Him, and how to live a life pleasing to Him. This kind of knowledge is foremost—we can't really live without it.

||||||||||||||||||||||||||||||||||||||||||||||||||||||||||||||||||||||||||||||||||||||||||||||||||||||||||||||||||||||||||||||||||||||||||||||||||||||||||||||

FIXER UPPER

As we complete our study on knowledge, we have concluded the great value which the Lord places on acquiring a knowledge of Him. This pursuit should be a matter of persistent and fervent prayer not only for ourselves but also for those we love. Take a few moments to pray these verses back to the Father asking Him to fill you and those you love with a knowledge of Him:

That the God of our Lord Jesus Christ, the Father of glory, may give to you a spirit of wisdom and of revelation in the knowledge of Him. I pray that the eyes of your heart may be enlightened, so that you will know what is the hope of His calling, what are the riches of the glory of His inheritance in the saints, and what is the surpassing greatness of His power toward us who believe. Ephesians 1:17-19a

And this I pray, that your love may abound still more and more in real knowledge and all discernment, so that you may approve the things that are excellent, in order to be sincere and blameless until the day of Christ; having been filled with the fruit of righteousness which comes through Jesus Christ, to the glory and praise of God. Philippians 1:9-11

For this reason also, since the day we heard of it, we have not ceased to pray for you and to ask that you may be filled with the knowledge of His will in all spiritual wisdom and understanding, so that you will walk in a manner worthy of the Lord, to please Him in all respects, bearing fruit in every good work and increasing in the knowledge of God. Colossians 1:9-10

Week 5
PRAYER

It happened that while Jesus was praying in a certain place, after He had finished, one of His disciples said to Him, "Lord, teach us to pray just as John also taught his disciples."

Luke 11:1

All of us know we should pray. Most of us feel guilty because we don't pray at all or enough. What can we do to move from duty to delight in our prayer lives? What has helped me most is praying with others who know how to pray. I have also enjoyed reading books by people of prayer. No one truly understands all that prayer is and does, but we do know it is the vehicle through which God has chosen to allow His will to come from heaven to earth.

When it comes right down to it, prayer is about relationship. It is about learning to hear the voice of the Lord through His Word and His Spirit, which helps us grow in intimacy with Him. As we get to know Him better, we love Him more and desire to spend more time with Him. What starts as a discipline turns into a lifeline of connection with the One Who knows you best and loves you the most. This week we are going to study prayer in the Bible. We will find out what the Bible has to say about it as well as learning from others who walked with God.

As we seek to fill our homes with the pleasant riches we have in Christ, there is no better place to start than with prayer. Praying through your home literally changes the atmosphere. Others will notice. His peace will prevail and your home will become the haven it was designed to be.

DAY ONE

What is Prayer?

Prayer is communion with God. It is how we get to know Him. Jeanne Guyon said, "Prayer is nothing but the application of the heart to God, and the internal exercise of love."[36]

1. Look up the following verses and summarize what they have to say about prayer:

    Genesis 20:17

Genesis 25:21

Numbers 11:1-2

1 Samuel 1:26-2

Psalm 141:2

Revelation 5:8; 8:3-4

Some Christians struggle with believing that God can answer prayer and intervene miraculously on our behalf. Not only does He move in response to our prayers, but He gathers them in golden bowls before His throne and they continually rise before Him as incense (Revelation 5:8). We say we believe in God, the very God who created the heavens and the earth (Genesis 1:1). If we are following and desiring to know this God, then we must be open to the supernatural.

As Tim Keller stated in his book, *Prayer: Experiencing Awe and Intimacy with God:*

> We are not called to choose between a Christian life based on truth and doctrine or a life filled with spiritual power and experience. They go together. I was not being called to leave behind my theology and launch out to look for 'something more,' for experience. Rather, I was meant to ask the Holy Spirit to help me experience my theology.[37]

2. Read 2 Kings 6:15-17. How did God answer the prayer of the prophet?

3a. Read 2 Kings 19:14-20. What is the context of God's miraculous answer?

3b. What do you do in times of trouble?

3c. What is your first resort?

As Oswald Chambers writes,

> Prayer is an interruption of personal ambition, and no person who is busy has time to pray. What will suffer is the life of God in him, which is nourished not by food but by prayer?[38]

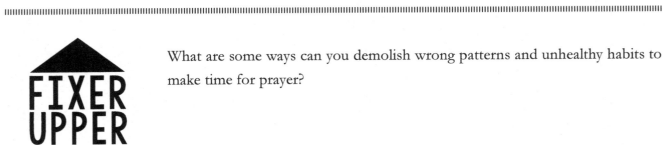

What are some ways can you demolish wrong patterns and unhealthy habits to make time for prayer?

How about not picking up your phone or opening your computer until after you have read the Bible and spent time in prayer? Maybe you need to go to bed a little earlier at night so you can get up and spend time with the Lord before going out into your day. How can you construct a time and a place where you will spend time in prayer? Where? When?

You must choose to make time with the Lord and plan for it. He is waiting for you.

DAY TWO

The Prayer Life of Jesus

The Bible is very clear that Jesus would often slip away and pray. In fact, after a very busy day of ministry in Mark 1:35 we find Jesus rising early, while it was still dark to find a secluded place to pray. If our Lord, who lived without sin, found it necessary to dedicate time with the Father, how much more diligent should you and I be about spending time with Him? The Gospel of Luke gives us great insight into the prayer life of Christ.

We are going to trace the prayer life of our Lord through this Gospel. I would encourage you to put a "P" in the margin every time prayer is mentioned.

1. Look up the following verses and write down a brief synopsis of what you learn about the prayer life of Jesus.

   Luke 3:21

   Luke 5:16

   Luke 6:12

77

Luke 6:28

Luke 9:18

In the NASB version of the Bible (which is a very literal translation) Luke 9:18 states, "And it happened that while He was praying alone, the disciples were with Him, and He questioned them, saying, 'Who do the people say that I am?'"

2. How was it that Christ was praying *alone* while the disciples were with Him?

One of my favorite women of history is Susanna Wesley, the mother of John and Charles Wesley. She gave birth to 19 children of whom only 10 survived to maturity. She was a devoted student of the Word, a pastor's wife and woman of prayer. She was a very structured woman who devoted time to the spiritual development of her children. She also spent time daily in prayer. Her children knew, when mother had her apron over her head, she was not to be disturbed. She was praying alone, while with her children. She once said, "I am content to fill a little space if God be glorified." So, moms, we don't have an excuse for not praying just because we have little ones in our home. We need to set aside a time and place to meet with Jesus *alone*, even if there are others around.

When our children were growing up, I set my alarm to get up about an hour before anyone else. This gave me time to spend reading the Bible and praying without being disturbed. As you know, if you have children, some of them will be early risers. When one of our children would wake before I had finished, I would give them a drink and cover them up on the couch beside me. I would continue to read or pray doing so out loud so they could hear me. This is a tremendous opportunity to model the priority of time with Jesus on a daily basis.

3. Read and summarize the following scriptures:

Luke 9:28-29

Luke 11:1-2

Don't you find it significant that the disciples requested that Jesus teach them to pray? It is the only such request they made of Him and is indicative of the fact that Christ's prayer life had profoundly impacted them and they desired to commune with the Father just as He did.

Are others drawn to Christ because of the evidence of Him in your life?

DAY THREE

The Prayer Life of Jesus

1a. Read the parable on prayer Jesus told in Luke 18:1-8. When Jesus comes will He find faith on the earth?

1b. To what was Jesus equating faith?

2. Read the following passages and summarize what you learn about prayer.

   Luke 18:10-11

   Luke 19:46

   Luke 20:46-47

Luke 21:36

Luke 22:40-46

We learn from the example of Christ the necessity of prayer. Tim Keller wrote, "The infallible test of spiritual integrity, Jesus says, is your private prayer life."[39]

Just as the disciples asked Jesus to teach them to pray, there have been people in my life that I have asked to teach me to pray. I have also learned about and been inspired by biographies about some of the great people of prayer throughout history. One of those people is John Hyde, lovingly referred to as "Praying Hyde."

Captain E. G. Carre, in the biography he wrote, relays a story that has gripped my heart. Evangelist Wilbur Chapman was holding services in England. The audiences had been small and unmoved. Hear what happened when John Hyde attended to intercede. These are Wilbur Chapman's own words:

> At one of our missions in England the audience was extremely small. Results seemed impossible, but I received a letter from a missionary that an American missionary known as 'Praying Hyde' would be in the place to pray God's blessing down upon our work. Almost instantly the tide changed – the hall was packed, and my first invitation meant fifty men for Jesus Christ. As we were leaving, I said, 'Mr. Hyde, I want you to pray for me.' He came to my room, turned the key in the door, dropped on his knees, waited five minutes without a single syllable coming from his lips. I could hear my own heart thumping and his beating. I felt the hot tears running down my face. I knew I was with God. Then with upturned face, down which tears streamed, he said, 'Oh God!' Then for five minutes at least he was still again, and then when he knew that he was talking to God, his arm went round my shoulder and then came up from the depth of his heart such petitions for men as I have never heard before, and I rose from my knees to know what real prayer was. We have gone round the world and back again, believing that prayer is mighty, and we believe it as never before.[40]

Oh, to know the Lord with such intimacy that our prayers would be energized by His Spirit and in tune with His will. May the Lord grant that our hearts would be wholly devoted to the Lord and His Kingdom. May our prayers be used by God to fill our homes and our churches with those who have come to Christ because of our prayers!

DAY FOUR

The Prayer Life of Paul

Paul was one of the greatest Christians to ever live. He wrote almost half of the New Testament under the inspiration of the Holy Spirit. As you read his epistles you will find multiple references to prayer. Paul's prayer life was the secret to his power and influence for the Kingdom of God.

1. Read Paul's prayer in Ephesians 1:15-19. Outline the specific things that he prays for the Ephesians.

2. What did he mean when he asked that the eyes of their heart would be enlightened?

We find that in all of Paul's prayers, he never asks for protection from enemies, deliverance from persecution or for the overthrow of the Roman government. But instead he prays that believers might know God more and that he might be bold in proclaiming the gospel.

3a. Read another prayer of Paul's in Ephesians 3:14-21. Outline the specific requests Paul made for the Ephesians.

3b. How did he close his prayer?

There are examples throughout history of those who have been faithful intercessors. It is to these that God grants extraordinary insight and spiritual conquests. One of my favorites is Monica, the mother of St. Augustine. Monica lived in the 4th century. She married at an early age and her husband was a pagan with a violent temper and lax morals. They had three children of whom Augustine was the oldest. Monica's gentle and quiet spirit eventually led to the salvation of her husband (AD 371) who died shortly after being accepted into the church.

Monica chose not to remarry and devoted herself to praying for her son who was living a rebellious and openly sinful life. She followed him to Milan. Monica cried out to God for his conversion. Once she turned to an unnamed bishop and pleading for advice, she received these words of wisdom: "Go your way; as you live, it cannot be that the son of these tears should perish."[41]

Augustine credits his mother as being the catalyst for his salvation. Through her earnest prayers for his soul, her consistent life of faith, and her unconditional love, he was converted. He was saved in 386 and baptized by Ambrose, Easter (April 25) 387. Little did Monica know as she prayed that God would not only answer her prayers but would also make her son one of the greatest early church fathers, who still impacts the church today.

3. Who are you praying for? How earnestly are you pleading for your loved one's salvation?

FIXER UPPER

Does your prayer life need a makeover?

Pause for a moment. Take out your prayer journal or notebook and make a list of lost loved ones. Begin today to pray daily for their salvation. Cry out to God on their behalf. Date the requests and when God answers, write down the date of His answer.

DAY FIVE

My Prayer Life

> "Prayer – secret, fervent, believing prayer – lies at the root of all personal godliness."[42]
> –E. M. Bounds

You can evaluate your intimacy with God by honestly evaluating your prayer life. How would you rate yours?

I have long been drawn to prayer and had a desire to walk and talk with the Lord. I have read many books about what it means to have a personal relationship with Christ and even wrote one about life in the Spirit. I have found that there is no real spiritual life apart from prayer. When Jesus was teaching His disciples in John 14-17 on the night before He was crucified, He explained to them the importance of abiding.

1. Read John 15:1-8. Make notes as God speaks to you through His Word.

2. Focus on John 15:7-8 – "If you abide in Me and My Words abide in you, ask whatever you wish, and it will be done for you. My Father is glorified by this, that you bear much fruit, and so prove to be My disciples."

As I was meditating on these verses one day, I suddenly realized that John 15:7 could be broken down into an acrostic for **ABIDE**:

Abandon - "If you abide in Me"

We must submit to and utterly abandon ourselves to Christ. This is how we make Him Lord of our lives and position ourselves to experience the fullness of His Spirit.

Believe – "and My Words abide in you"

We must believe God's Word. To believe it, we must read it and know it. That is why it is so important to have a plan for reading through God's Word each year and also a time and place dedicated to spending time with Him.

Intercede – "ask"

It is only after we have abandoned ourselves to Christ and take Him at His Word that we are ready to intercede according to His will.

Delight – "whatever you wish"

Psalms tells us to "Delight yourself in the Lord and He will give you the desires of your heart" (Psalm 37:4). To delight ourselves in Him, means we make ourselves soft and pliable in His hands. It is as we are conformed into His image (Romans 12:2) that His desires become our desires.

Expect – "it will be done for you"

We must place our faith in God's Word and His desire to answer out prayers. Our job is to believe. Hebrews 11:6 tells us it is impossible to please Him without faith.

3. John 15:8 begins by saying: "My Father is glorified by this…" To what is Christ referring?

4. Answered prayer is proof that we are His disciples. If that is proof, is there enough proof (answered prayers) that you belong to Christ?

Prayer is the key to intimacy and bearing the fruit of the Spirit. It is essential for spiritual growth and maturity. As Tim Keller said in his book, *Prayer: Experiencing Awe and Intimacy with God*:

> Prayer is the only entryway into genuine self-knowledge. It is also the main way we experience deep change – the reordering of our lives. Prayer is how God gives us so many of the unimaginable things he has for us. Indeed, prayer makes it safe for God to give us many of the things we most desire. It is the way we know God, the way we finally treat God as God. Prayer is simply the key to everything we need to do and be in life. We must learn to pray. We have to![43]

Week 6
FRUIT

But the Holy Spirit produces this kind of fruit in our lives:
love, joy, peace, patience, kindness, goodness, faithfulness, gentleness, and self-control.
Galatians 5:22-23a (NLT)

The purpose for your occupying space and taking up oxygen, your reason for existence, is to bear fruit. If you are not bearing fruit, there is no reason for your existence. The Word says that if you want to glorify the Father, you will bear fruit. If you want to demonstrate that you are His disciple, you will bear fruit. If you want to be a blessing to the world, you will bear fruit. [44]
—W. Oscar Thompson, Jr.

DAY ONE

1. Refer back to John 15:1-12. (We looked at this passage last week.) What does this parable teach us about bearing fruit? According to these verses, how do we bear fruit?

2. What are the results of bearing spiritual fruit (v. 7, 11)?

"Abide in Me." These are Jesus' words to believers in John 15:4. Before we bear fruit, we must abide. Merriam-Webster's definition of abide is "to remain stable or fixed in a state, to continue in a place, to conform to, to accept without objection."[45] So consider this in light of our relationship with our Savior. Remain stable in Him. Be fixed on Him. Continue with Him. Conform to Him. Accept Him without objection.

Before we dive into the specifics of the fruit of the Spirit, let us examine Scripture to better understand what it looks like to abide.

3a. Read John 5:19. What do we see in the life of Jesus?

3b. How can this be applied in your life?

Thompson goes on to say, "Jesus was in total submission to and in union with the Father. As a result of that submission, the Father manifested His character in Jesus. Jesus came to earth not only to die for us but also to manifest the character of the Father so that people can see what God is like."[46]

The world is watching. Your family is watching. As Christians, we were created to and are called to reflect the image of our Heavenly Father with the hope of bringing others to a saving knowledge of Jesus Christ. A branch securely attached to the vine results in the production of beautiful fruit.

4. What might stand in your way of staying connected to the Vine? As an individual? As a family or household?

5. What might God prune in your life that will help you be more fruitful? How can you reconnect and abide in Him?

This fruit (Galatians 5:22-23) is the manifestation of God's character as a result of abiding in Him and Him in us. The Holy Spirit produces this fruit as a result of our submission to and union with the Father. Let's begin looking at the fruit of the Spirit, one by one, and considering how we can infuse these into the atmosphere of our homes.

Today, we will consider love. It is listed first in the fruit of the Spirit. Make no mistake. We cannot bear the fruit of the Spirit without love. This aspect must be in its proper place so that the others can build upon it and flow from it. Love is the foundation. As with a house, if the foundation is nonexistent or unsteady, the house will crumble.

6. What are the characteristics of God's love? What does the Bible teach us about love?

John 3:16

John 13:34-35

Ephesians 5:1-2

Romans 5:8

1 John 4:19

1 John 4:8 tells us, "God is love." If we need a clear example of how to love, we need to look no further than God Himself. He IS love. His love is unconditional, sacrificial, selfless and enduring. If we are abiding in Him and allowing the Holy Spirit to produce fruit in our lives, we will be channels of His love. We will love unconditionally, sacrificially, selflessly and with endurance.

7. Consider those in your home (or in your sphere of influence). How can you love like this? In what ways can you practically live this out at home?

8. Search the Bible to see the scope of God's love. The Bible calls us to love as God loves (John 13:34). Describe God's love and consider how you can demonstrate love, within your home, as He loves.

   Revelation 7:9 (breadth of His love) –

   Ephesians 1:4-5 (length of His love) –

   Ephesians 2:6 (height of His love) –

   2 Corinthians 5:21 (depth of His love) –

Love is the result of yielding to God and setting self aside with the hope and intention of practicing Biblical love in our homes. Love gives freely, without condition and without expectation of anything in return. Are you motivated, determined, disciplined, and committed to love others as Christ loves you? Make a fresh commitment today to exemplify and imitate the love the Father has lavished on us. You may ask, "What is the secret to imitating the love of the Father?"

Behold the Savior.

> Help me never to forget, Lord, that this is where I need to be – near to the cross, **beholding my Savior**. For this is the fountain where love is most pure. This is where I am cleansed, not only from my sin but from my pettiness. This is where I am closest to you. This is where I am closest to those who love you. Bring me here daily, Lord. **This is where love is**. And this is where I need to be…(emphasis mine). [47]

Ask the Lord to release love, the fruit of HIS Spirit, into the atmosphere of your home. This is the foundation on which the others are built. Let it begin with you.

DAY TWO

Based upon his study of Scripture, Rick Warren says, "Joy is the settled assurance that God is in control of all the details of my life, the quiet confidence that ultimately everything is going to be alright, and the determined choice to praise God in every situation."[48]

The next fruit of the Spirit we'll examine is joy. We tend to think of joy and happiness synonymously. However, as we look into Scripture, we see there is a distinct difference. I love how Rick Warren speaks of it as a "settled assurance," "quiet confidence," and "determined choice." Happiness comes and goes. It depends on our present circumstances and fluctuates day to day, sometimes moment by moment. As the psalmist writes in Psalm 33:20-22, our hearts should **brim** with joy because we have exchanged our name for His name. Let that sink in for a moment. This alone should result in unspeakable, unwavering, undeniable joy in the life of every child of God.

> We're depending on God; he's everything we need. What's more, our hearts brim with joy since we've taken for our own his holy name. Love us, God, with all you've got — that's what we're depending on. Psalm 33:20-22 (MSG)

Reflecting back on Day One, we were reminded that our fruit bearing comes as a result of abiding in Him. We cannot bear fruit apart from Him. Therefore, we cannot produce and experience joy apart from God. If we are truly depending on Him for <u>everything</u>, connected to and nourished by the Vine, we will experience joy! It will not be dependent upon our circumstances. It will be settled and we will be confident. Then, we can determine in our hearts to choose joy!

1. How does joy satisfy? (1 Peter 1:8-9)

2. How do we experience joy? (Psalm 16:11; Psalm 119:1-3; Psalm 1:1-2; Romans 15:13)

3. Is joy a command, a matter of obedience? (Philippians 4:4; Psalm 32:11; James 1:2-4)

Happiness is temporary and dependent on circumstances. Joy is supernatural and lasting. Amy Carmichael says, "There is nothing dreary and doubtful about life. It is meant to be continually joyful.... We are called to a settled happiness in the Lord whose joy is our strength."[49]

4. Take a few moments to answer these questions and ask the Holy Spirit to shine a spotlight on your heart. Do your perspectives or priorities need realigning with God's Truth so you can experience true joy?

   - What is important to you? How do you spend your time? Where do you find your worth? (Consider man's approval versus God's approval.)

   - How big is your God? How do you view Him in the midst of crisis?

   - Do your children/grandchildren see joy in you? Does it permeate your life? How can you better demonstrate joy in your daily life?

God is such a God of detail. I love this about His character. As Paul lists the fruit of the Spirit in Galatians 5, I find it interesting that love is first, which is the foundation upon which we build. Next comes joy which we should experience because of the love He has demonstrated toward us (Romans 5:8). Then, we come to peace. Close your eyes for a moment. Get still and quiet. Pause and whisper the word "peace." Doesn't the mere mention of it give your heart a sense of calm and stillness?

Not only is God a God of detail, but He is also a God of perfect timing. Just a couple of hours before I sat down to pen the words for today's study, my mom sent me a text message with this verse: "I listen carefully to what God the LORD IS SAYING, FOR HE SPEAKS PEACE TO HIS FAITHFUL PEOPLE. BUT LET THEM NOT RETURN TO THEIR FOOLISH WAYS" (Psalm 85:8, NLT).

5. According to this scripture, to whom is peace promised?

My mom shared these thoughts on this promise from God's Word.

> All God has to do is speak peace, but notice to whom He speaks it. I cannot receive God's peace and then think I have a patent on it for the rest of my life regardless of the path I take. God speaks peace to His <u>faithful</u> people. I cannot expect God's peace apart from my faithfulness. If I desire God's peace in my life, I am not to return to my foolish ways. So today, I pray, "God, may I have a listening heart, an obedient heart, a wise heart and a faithful heart. Then I <u>know</u> You will speak peace to it because Your Word promises it.

Imagine sitting in a large group and hearing the question, "Who would like peace to rule in your home?" I am confident every single hand would go up. We long for peace in a world so full of unrest. We long for peace in homes where there can sometimes be chaos and strife. We long for peace in relationships where hurts and differences exist. As a child of God, we have a responsibility to listen, to be faithful and to be obedient.

6. Read John 16:33. In the midst of trials and sorrow, what can we have <u>in</u> Jesus? Why?

Perhaps you are working through the pages of today's study thinking, "Oh, how desperately I want peace in my heart. I want to bear this fruit and see it fill my home." Praise be to God because He alone is the Provider of Peace. In Mark 4:39, Jesus said to the stormy sea, "'Peace! Be still!' And the wind ceased, and there was a great calm" (ESV). He is the same God today as He was in Mark 4. He desires to hold out His hand over your life, your family, your home and say, "Peace! Be still!"

In John 14, Jesus promises the gift of the Holy Spirit to His disciples as He would soon leave them and return to heaven. This same gift is given to all who believe and call on the name of the Lord Jesus Christ for salvation. If you are in Jesus Christ, you can claim and stand on this promise. "Peace I leave with you; my peace I give you. I do not give to you as the world gives. Do not let your hearts be troubled and do not be afraid" (John 14:27, NIV).

7a. Read Philippians 4:6-7. What four instructions are given here (v. 6)?

7b. What is the result of obeying these commands (v. 7)?

7c. What does His peace do for us (v. 7)?

To never worry about anything seems impossible, doesn't it? To our human, finite minds, it is. The Bible tells us, "For no matter how many promises God has made, they are 'Yes' in Christ" (2 Corinthians 1:20a, NIV). If He has said it, we can count on it! According to Philippians 4:6, we need to turn our worry into prayer. Do you want to worry less? Then pray more!

Ask the Lord to release joy and peace, the fruit of HIS Spirit, into the atmosphere of your home.

As you consider the scriptures we've examined today, how will you plan to infuse your home with joy and peace? Ask yourself these questions:

- Am I experiencing a life of joy on a regular basis, or is my happiness dependent on things going smoothly in my day?

- Do I find myself frazzled by the crashing waves of turmoil in my life, or am I experiencing "the peace of God, which surpasses all comprehension" (Philippians 4:7)?

Share any insight with your small group.

"You will keep in perfect peace all who trust in You, all whose thoughts are fixed on You!"
Isaiah 26:3, (NLT)

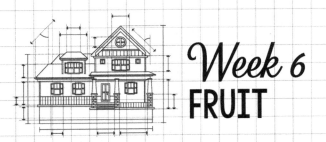

DAY THREE

In 1 Corinthians 13:4a Paul writes, "Love is patient and kind" (NLT).

Do you find it interesting that patience and kindness are the first words Paul used to explain love? These are also the next fruit of the Spirit that we come to in this week's study. Let's dig in!

In her book, *Own Your Life*, Sally Clarkson says, "Whether you are single or married, young or old, painting the reality of God onto the walls of your home will be one of the great works of your life. People long for holy shelter: a safe place of comfort that values and preserves all that is good and offers solace from all the pain life's issues can bring."[50]

Holy shelter. What a thought. Through obedience, abiding in Jesus and, as a result, producing fruit that comes from His Spirit, I can create a holy shelter for my family and for those who enter the walls of my home. What a responsibility! What a privilege!

As we consider building our homes for the glory of God, let's closely examine patience. Did anyone else just cringe? This one seems to be a hard one for most of us. We, in general, are not a patient people. We want fast. Fast food. Quick service. Speedy internet. Instant downloads. We want it now! This is the world in which we live. Our Heavenly Father has called us, though, to look different from this world. He calls us to be transformed rather than conformed to the patterns of this world (Romans 12:2). I cannot think of a better way to be set apart than to exhibit a life of patience.

R. C. Sproul says, "When the Bible speaks of patience, particularly as one of the fruits of the Spirit, and as one of the characteristics of love, it speaks of it as a virtue that goes far beyond the mere ability to await some future gain. It involves more than the rest or peace of the soul that trusts in God's perfect timing. The patience that is in view here focuses more on interpersonal relationships with other people."[51]

1. Let's dig into the Bible to see what God says about patience. Consider how you can apply these to your interpersonal relationships, primarily those within your home.

   Proverbs 14:29

Galatians 6:9

Isaiah 30:18

Ephesians 4:2

James 5:7

I confess that I often fall short in the patience arena…more than I'd like to admit. Would you agree that we, as women, often feel justified in our impatience? Seriously, think about it. Husbands need us. Children need us. Continually. We are the question answerer. We maintain the home, do the laundry, clean up messes, drive carpool, manage the calendar, help with homework, cook meals, pack lunches, soothe booboo's, console hurt feelings. And the list goes on and on. Maybe you're a bit like me and your heart begins to palpitate just reading through that list. How can we possibly be patient in the midst of all of this?

Home is the residence of those we love the most. Love is patient, so this would suggest that patience should be a priority in our homes. When something is at the top of our priority list, we are committed to it, determined to tend to it and do it well. Is this your mindset toward being patient?

2a. In what areas in the home, do you struggle with patience? What steps have you taken (or plan to take) to deal with impatience?

2b. Have you claimed specific scriptures to help you?

In the list of the fruit of the Spirit, kindness follows patience. Again, I do not find this coincidental but rather as proof of God's intimate knowledge of His creation. If I am impatient, I am unkind. If I display patience, especially in the face of suffering or difficulty, I demonstrate kindness. Think about it. If your sweet little one asks for a drink of water and then asks 27 more times, you are likely to feel the patient meter running out? When this happens (and we all know it does), how do you respond?

Patience and kindness go hand in hand. I ran across "Daily Treasures" from *Love Worth Finding Ministries with Adrian Rogers* in recent reading. I pray you enjoy these excerpts and soak up the truths he shares about kindness in the home.

> Do you know where we need to be kind the most? In our homes. Why is it that sometimes we are the most unkind to those we love the best? The most cutting remarks sometimes occur in the home. Indeed, there are many marriages that could be saved by a little gentleness.
>
> The psalmist said of the Lord, "Thou hast also given me the shield of Thy salvation: and Thy gentleness hath made me great" (2 Samuel 22:36).
>
> Are you a mother and want your children to be great? Be gentle. They will grow and blossom with a father and mother who are gentle. The Bible says of a wife: "She openeth her mouth with wisdom; and in her tongue is the law of kindness" (Proverbs 31:26). Your children need this kindness perhaps more than anything else.[52]

3. How does your heart respond as you read Proverbs 31:26? When you open your mouth, is the teaching of kindness on your tongue? (Commit this verse to memory. Pray it daily. Pray it in the moment as you are considering the words with which you are about to speak.)

Sometimes busyness stands in the way of being kind. As women, we can relate to and understand busyness. We all experience busyness in one way or the other. This is not limited to any specific age group or role. If you are a woman, you are busy tending to something and/or someone.

Dr. Adrian Rogers goes on to say,

> The chief enemy to kindness is busyness. We have our priorities, our jobs, our duties, our responsibilities…we're too busy. But if we are too busy to be kind, we are too busy. The Bible says: "As we have therefore opportunity, let us do good unto all men, especially unto them who are of the household of faith" (Galatians 6:10).
>
> Do you remember the story of the Good Samaritan? In Luke chapter 10, our Lord tells the story of a man on a journey who stopped to help a bruised and bleeding man on the side of the road.
>
> He didn't make excuses because he was on a journey and too busy to stop. He didn't say it was too dangerous to help a stranger. He didn't say it was none of his business. Right when he saw him, he didn't hesitate. He did what he could do. It was a golden moment – and he took it.
>
> All around us are people who are bruised and bleeding. Some are bleeding financially, some emotionally, and some spiritually. And they need you to say, "This is a golden opportunity to help someone, and I'm going to take it right now."
>
> "And be ye kind one to another, tenderhearted, forgiving one another, even as God for Christ's sake hath forgiven you." (Ephesians 4:32) [53]

4. While this account from Scripture doesn't speak to a familial relationship, how can you apply these principles to your home life and those that live or visit there?

5. Am I easily set off when things go wrong or people irritate me, or am I able to keep a godly perspective in the face of life's irritations?

6. Is it my goal to serve others with kindness, or am I too focused on my own needs, desires, or problems to let the goodness of God overflow to others?

||||||||||||||||||||||||||||||||||||||||||||||||||||||||||||||||||||||||||||||||||||||||||||||||||||||||||||||||||||||||||||||||||||||||||||||||||||||||||||||||||||||||

FIXER UPPER

Consider writing these verses out on a notecard. Discuss them at the dinner table and come up with ideas, as a family, on how you can display kindness in your home according to God's Word.

Proverbs 11:16-17

Proverbs 12:25

Jeremiah 9:24

Luke 6:31

1 Thessalonians 5:15

1 John 3:18

Ask the Lord to release patience and kindness, the fruit of HIS Spirit, into the atmosphere of your home.

And then, go! Go and live out the patience and kindness of Jesus Christ to a world in need of a Savior!

||||||||||||||||||||||||||||||||||||||||||||||||||||||||||||||||||||||||||||||||||||||||||||||||||||||||||||||||||||||||||||||||||||||||||||||||||||||||||||||||||||||||

Week 6
FRUIT

DAY FOUR

Merriam-Webster defines goodness as "the quality or state of being good; the nutritious, flavorful or beneficial part of something."[54] This sounds like a reasonable and accurate description, doesn't it?

Let us continue our study of the fruit of the Spirit, and look at God's definition of goodness.

The Greek word translated "goodness," *agathosune*, is defined as "uprightness of heart and life." This would imply a virtue of righteousness and holiness. How is this possible? Can we muster up goodness by our own effort?

As we have seen in this week's study, apart from Jesus, we can do <u>nothing</u> (John 15:5). We are unable to bear fruit unless we are attached to the Vine. He is the Producer. We are the bearer. Anything good comes from our Father (James 1:17) and any fruit we bear comes from His Spirit. Goodness is no exception.

1. The world tells us that people are innately good and often denies that mankind is born with a sinful nature. What does Jeremiah 17:9 say in response to this line of thinking?

The Life Application Bible notes, "God makes it clear why we sin – it's a matter of the heart. Our heart is inclined toward sin from the time we are born. It is easy to fall into the routine of forgetting and forsaking God."[55]

Just as he did in the garden, Satan would have us believe the opposite of the truth in God's Word so that we avoid personal responsibility and accountability for our sin. Our hearts are not naturally good. We all (and that means all) fall short of God's glory (Romans 3:23) and can bear nothing good apart from Jesus Christ.

2. Read Mark 10:18. According to Jesus' response to the rich young ruler, who is truly good?

3. Take a look at the following verses. What do they teach about goodness? How can you practically teach these truths to your children/grandchildren? (If you are single, how can you impart and live out this truth to those with whom you spend time?)

Luke 6:45

Ephesians 5:8-10

2 Thessalonians 1:11

As Joshua Straub notes,

> The 'goodness' described as a fruit of the Spirit is not merely moral behavior, but an excellence of character. It combines our attempts to do good with God's character of being good. This goodness is only attainable through God's divine power at work in our hearts (2 Peter 1:3). This means that simply teaching our children to do good can look very much like legalism. The rich young ruler was trying to do good to earn his way into heaven, yet he was lacking the most important thing — an underlying love for the Rule Maker. This love is what compels us to follow the rules in the first place (2 Corinthians 5:14). Goodness begins by obeying the greatest commandment of an all-loving God with all our heart, soul and strength. As we love God, He works His character of goodness into our lives.[56]

4. Has your perspective on "goodness" changed any as you've studied today?

Just as faithfulness follows goodness in the fruit of the Spirit, we should progress toward faithfulness as we dwell on the goodness of God and then, in turn, practice that goodness toward others. Perhaps this will help us experience and know more deeply the essence of faithfulness, both the faithfulness of God and our faithfulness to Him. In *Mere Christianity*, C.S. Lewis says, "We have to be continually reminded of what we believe. Neither this belief nor any other will automatically remain alive in the mind. It must be fed."[57]

5. Let's feed our minds with the truth of God's Word. What do these verses teach about the faithfulness of God? How do these verses minister to your heart personally?

Deuteronomy 7:9

Psalm 86:15

Lamentations 3:22-23

Psalm 91:4

We are image bearers of God, therefore, we should look like Him. As we consider His faithfulness to us, I pray we are challenged to be a people of faith and look more and more like Him. Faith is believing Him and trusting Him…no matter what. Hebrews 11 tells us that faith is the assurance of things we hope for, the evidence of what we cannot see (v. 1) and that it is impossible to please God without it (v. 6).

Faith is like a muscle in that it has to be used to remain strong. We need to use it and allow God to grow and strengthen it just as a muscle strengthens from disciplined exercise and work.

Kurt Bruner says this of building faith in the home:

Practice faithfulness, though, and you will provide stability, security and confidence for your children. You will reflect God to them. And you will instill in them the importance of being true to their word. When your children develop faithful hearts, they will stay in a close walk with God; they will also find more success in their schoolwork, their friendships, their marriage and their career. Remember: Faithfulness is an attribute of the fruit of the Spirit, empowered by God. So pray for it. Model it. Teach it. Celebrate it.[58]

6. Read these verses and record your thoughts as it relates to faith in us.

Proverbs 28:20

Matthew 25:21

2 Corinthians 5:7

Proverbs 3:3-4

As Richard Strauss comments,

> When we are assured that He cares because He is loving and good; when we are convinced that He is in control because He is omnipotent; when we believe that He is with us and knows all about the problem because He is omnipresent and omniscient; when we believe that He is working everything together for good because He is sovereign and wise; then we will have peace when things around us are falling apart. And that will make a powerful impact on the world.[59]

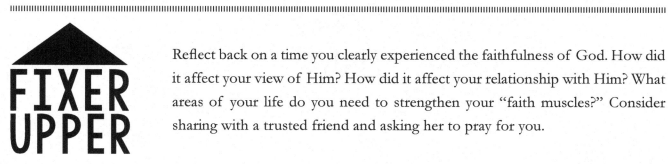

FIXER UPPER

Reflect back on a time you clearly experienced the faithfulness of God. How did it affect your view of Him? How did it affect your relationship with Him? What areas of your life do you need to strengthen your "faith muscles?" Consider sharing with a trusted friend and asking her to pray for you.

Ask the Lord to release goodness and faithfulness, the fruit of HIS Spirit, into the atmosphere of your home.

The unfailing love of the LORD never ends! His mercies never cease. Great is his faithfulness...
The LORD is good to those who depend on him, to those who search for him."
Lamentations 3:22-23a, 25 (NLT)

DAY FIVE

Jonathan Edwards said, "All who are truly godly and are real disciples of Christ have a gentle spirit in them."[60]

Paul says in 1 Thessalonians 2:7, "We were gentle among you, like a mother caring for her little children" (NIV). Does this mean that Paul and his companions were immature or untrained? Not at all. Rather, it shows that as they presented the truth of the Gospel to the young believers in Thessalonica, they were honest and straightforward as well as encouraging and comforting. He did not share the truth bashfully, yet he did it with gentleness.

This teaches that we can speak truth to others, including those within the walls of our home, and still exhibit this fruit of the Spirit. Gentleness is displaying a strong hand with a soft touch, dealing with the weaknesses of others with care and compassion yet without compromise.

1.   Let's look at a beautiful example of this in John 8:1-11. What happens to the woman in the story and how does Jesus respond? Does He ignore her sin? How might she have responded/reacted differently if Jesus' response had been harsh?

In typical fashion, the devil and the world would have us believe gentleness equals weakness. This could not be further from the truth in God's Word. God's Word admonishes us, commands us, to be gentle and that it be evident to all...even those with whom we disagree. This controlled strength displays the character of Jesus Christ and causes the world to take note of the difference He makes in our lives.

2. Read Galatians 6:1. In light of this verse and the account from John 8, how should we respond to the sins or weaknesses of others?

3a. What phrases in Psalm 23:1-3 reflect the gentleness of God as our Shepherd?

3b. How can you emulate God as you shepherd the hearts of your children/grandchildren or those over whom you have influence?

God is overwhelmingly gentle with me when I mess up. I sense a gentle, quiet nudge from His heart to mine as He brings conviction that leads to change and a restored relationship. Am I responding with that same gentleness to others? As I attach myself to the Vine and allow the truth of His word to nourish me, the branch, I will bear the fruit of gentleness.

Max Lucado says, "I choose gentleness…Nothing is won by force. I choose to be gentle. If I raise my voice, may it be only in praise. If I clench my fist, may it be only in prayer. If I make a demand, may it be only of myself."[61]

Gentleness can also be translated as meekness. Take time to read through these thoughts from John Piper and journal your thoughts as you go. Where do you see weak spots in your life and in your home?

> Meekness begins when we put our trust in God. Then, because we trust him, we commit our way to him. We roll onto him our anxieties, our frustrations, our plans, our relationships, our jobs, our health.

And then we wait patiently for the Lord. We trust his timing and his power and his grace to work things out in the best way for his glory and for our good.

The result of trusting God, and the rolling of our anxieties onto God, and waiting patiently for him is that we don't give way to quick and fretful anger. But instead, we give place to wrath and hand our cause over to God and let him vindicate us if he chooses.

And then, as James says, in this quiet confidence we are slow to speak and quick to listen (James 1:19). We become reasonable and open to correction (James 3:17). James calls this the 'meekness of wisdom' (James 3:13).

Meekness loves to learn. And it counts the corrective blows of a friend as precious (Proverbs 27:6). And when it must say a critical word to a person caught in sin or error, it speaks from the deep conviction of its own fallibility and its own susceptibility to sin and its utter dependence on the grace of God (Galatians 6:1).

The quietness and openness and vulnerability of meekness is very beautiful and very painful. It goes against all that we are by our sinful nature. It requires supernatural help.

If you are a disciple of Jesus Christ — if you trust him and commit your way to him and wait patiently for him — God has already begun to help you and will help you even more.

And the primary way that he will help you is to assure your heart that you are a fellow heir of Jesus Christ and that the world and everything in it is yours (1 Corinthians 3:21–23). The meek inherit the earth (Matthew 5:5). [62]

As I mentioned earlier, I find it interesting how God orders the fruit. He lays them all out for us and they seem to build upon one another. The bookend of the list is self-control. Woah…that's a big one! And all the chocolate lovers said, "Amen!"

I once read that practicing self-control in the life of a believer is choosing Christ over the world. We do this by obeying Luke 9:23 (NIV) which says, "Whoever wants to be my disciple must deny themselves and take up their cross daily and follow me."

We keep in step with His Spirit when we exhibit self-control. We will take a more in-depth look at this virtue later in our study.

One of my most precious mentors gave me this nugget of wisdom. She would pray often for the Lord to release the fruit of the Spirit into the atmosphere of her home. She would walk through her home, with hands raised, and ask Him to fill it so that every person who entered in would know the Spirit of the Lord was in that place. I encourage you to do the same.

Begin each day with this prayer:

"Lord God, will you come and fill the very atmosphere of my home with the fruit of Your Spirit…love, joy, peace, patience, kindness, goodness, faithfulness, gentleness and self-control… and let me be a vessel from which they flow."

It is the Spirit who gives life; the flesh profits nothing. The words that I speak to you are spirit, and they are life.
John 6:63 (NKJV)

Week 7
ROLES

God created man in His own image, in the image of God He created him; male and female He created them.

Genesis 1:27

As we begin our study of man and woman, their creation and purpose, perhaps we could borrow a line from the score of *The Sound of Music,* "Let's start at the very beginning, a very good place to start." This week we will consider the creation narrative found in Genesis that starts, "In the beginning God created the heavens and the earth" (Genesis 1:1). And what follows is a magnificent rendering of the creation story. By a mere spoken word from our creative God, the universe was formed. Day after day, he carefully designed each detail—day and night, land and water and sky, plants and trees, sun and moon and stars, fish and birds, animals of every kind—according to His plan. Then on the sixth day, God crafted his crowning creation, man, and breathed into him the breath of life, making him distinctive from the rest of creation.

> Now came the moment to which all creation was leading—the creation of man in God's image. Everything that had gone before was subordinate to this. The world had been made for mankind.[63]

With this in mind, let's delve into the familiar story to see what insight we can glean about mankind, both man and woman, and how they fit into God's purpose. It's an amazing chronicle of grace.

DAY ONE

In the creation narrative, we observe the earth progress, within the span of a chapter, from a formless, dark void into a teeming planet filled with life and beauty under the hand of our mighty God. According to Genesis 1, this transpired within the space of six days. Now commentators sometimes disagree as to whether this was a literal six days, but we can conclude that it took place according to His divine timetable.

Because of the familiarity of these passages, we might be tempted skim over the account. But today let's focus in on the details to discover a truth which we may have missed or forgotten.

1. Read Genesis 1. Name three recurring phrases that you find in the passage. What do these phrases reveal to you about God?

2. Review Genesis 1:26-2:25. Look for specifics regarding the creation of both man and woman and list them below.

   Man

   Woman

3. Who was created first?

4. What materials were used in the creation of man and woman? Do you derive any significance from the details of their creation?

It is interesting to note that the Hebrew word for man is *adam* (which is frequently used in Scripture to denote a more generic mankind including both man and woman) and the Hebrew word for ground is *adamah*. This play on words is a reminder of God's building material for mankind. Since woman was created from the man, she also hails from the dust of the earth. Yet there is something more that differentiates mankind from the animals.

5. What two significant facts separate mankind from the animals? (vs. 1:27, 2:7)

6. Meditate on the concept that you were created in the very image of God. Should this realization change the way you view life and the way you live day by day? Write your thoughts.

7. How did Adam respond after the creation of Eve?

8. What assignment did God give Adam? What was Eve's responsibility?

Alexander Strauch presents a poignant description of God's provision for Adam by the creation of Eve:

> Eve was not another male; she was not a clone of Adam nor was she a twin. She was similar but different. She had her own biology, physiology, and psychology. She was made to complement man, to help him populate and rule the earth, and to unite with him as a loving companion-partner. This is the first statement in the Bible concerning the woman's role; she is to be a help to the man.[64]

With the arrival of Eve, we catch a glimpse of God's divine plan for His creation—marriage.

And so, we see Adam and Eve in the idyllic garden sharing fellowship with God Himself—who could ask for more. Mary Kassian and Nancy Leigh DeMoss describe it beautifully:

> The first male and female experienced what God created the closest of all human relationships to be. Their kinship was perfect. Their commitment was perfect. Their unity was perfect. Their communion was perfect. They were perfectly authentic and pure. Their relationship was paradise![65]

But quite frankly, we know the rest of the story—tune in tomorrow for trouble in paradise!

FIXER UPPER

Today we have viewed God as the great Creator who proclaimed that His creation was good—perfect in every way. Yet as women, sometimes we view our own personal creation as less than perfect. As I was reflecting on this, my mind went back to my high school years when all the guys would gather at my house to talk about how much they loved my friend, Starlene. All of their adulation would lead a girl to think: if only I were as beautiful, as smart, as graceful, as tall, as talented as Starlene. Perhaps you have a similar story. But the truth is that God was very intentional about your creation—He made you exactly according to His purpose and it was good.

Whenever the enemy comes to call to discourage you in the area of self-esteem, meditate on these familiar verses from Psalm 139:13-16 for a good reminder of the care your Creator God took in fashioning you.

> For You formed my inward parts; You wove me in my mother's womb. I will give thanks to You, for I am fearfully and wonderfully made; wonderful are Your works, and my soul knows it very well. My frame was not hidden from You, when I was made in secret, and skillfully wrought in the depths of the earth; Your eyes have seen my unformed substance; and in Your book were all written the days that were ordained for me, when as yet there was not one of them.

Wonderfully made—I'll go with that!

Week 7
ROLES

DAY TWO

As we completed our study yesterday in the creation narrative, we left Adam and Eve in the perfect environment living companionably with one another while fellowshipping with God. It was a flawless setting, but as Genesis 3 opens, we see a potential catastrophe enter the garden in the form of a serpent. It seems entirely innocent at first as the serpent engages Eve in conversation, but it quickly progresses into a dialogue that portends dire results. Even though we reviewed this passage in Week 2, let's remind ourselves of the details.

1. Read Genesis 3 to refresh your memory of Satan's temptation of Eve. Record any insights that you gain from this account.

The next scene presents Adam and Eve hiding from the presence of God. Where once they had interacted comfortably with God, now they shied away from Him because of their sin. God questioned Adam and eventually the truth was revealed and the relationship changed forever. Notice that God asked Adam for an explanation rather than Eve even though she was the one who had succumbed to Satan's temptation. He was the designated leader and responsible for what transpired in the garden. What happened next could literally be called the blame game.

2. What was Adam's response to God's question?

3.   How did Eve explain herself?

In *Divine Design*, the authors note:

> Adam and Eve may have been the first, but they certainly weren't the last in what has become a long, unbroken line of "blame-shifters." When we are angry, depressed, bitter, annoyed, impatient, or fearful, our natural response is to shift at least some of the responsibility onto the people or circumstances that we think "made" us that way.

> Broken communion between God and man immediately resulted in broken communion between man and woman. Their unity was severely damaged. It was no longer, "We're in this together!" Instead, sin poisoned them with the attitude, "Every man for himself!" and "Every woman for herself!" [66]

Along with sin came betrayal and severe consequences not only affecting them individually but all of future mankind. We each live in the shadow of their sin.

4.   List sin's consequences for both Adam and Eve. (Genesis 3:16-19)

God's original design for man and woman was in His heart long before the fall. He created them to complement one another rather than compete with one another. Man was to be the leader, provider and protector. Woman was to be his helper and the means through whom they would multiply and fill the earth. God's plan never changed but His judgment on sin made it more difficult for man and woman to accomplish His purpose—because we inherited our sin nature from Adam.

Mary Kassian and Nancy Leigh DeMoss describe the aftermath of sin like this:

> Sin twisted the positive desire of woman to respond amenably to man into a negative desire to resist and rebel against him.
>
> Sin twisted the positive drive of man to use his strength to lead, protect, and provide for woman into a negative tendency to abuse her or to abdicate his responsibility toward her.[67]

So, we now see what has often been called the battle of the sexes. In my lifetime, I have watched as the culture has become increasingly more hostile toward marriage and the traditional, biblical roles of men and women. As a wife and mother of two adult sons, I have developed an increasing frustration about the derogatory manner in which men are portrayed in the media thus influencing the way society thinks about them. I believe that much of this decline has its roots in feminism.

I am a child of the sixties—no doubt I am dating myself here! My first introduction to feminism occurred while I was in college. As an English major, I was enrolled in a Modern Literature class when my professor asked me to review a book called *The Feminine Mystique* by Betty Friedan. In her book, Mrs. Friedan sought to redefine womanhood and escape the traditional roles of women which she called the mystique. In 1966, the National Organization for Women was founded by Betty Friedan and a few others and the Women's Liberation movement was on its way. In just a few years, radios were blaring Helen Reddy's song, "I Am Woman," while countless women sang along. Soon, Women's Studies programs made their way onto college campuses, and women's issues such as abortion were being debated on the national stage. And the culture began to change—at a rapid pace, actually.

Mary Kassian and Nancy Leigh Demoss commented on feminism in their book, *Divine Design*,

> Feminism, as a cultural movement, has tapered off. This is not to say feminism has ended. On the contrary. The only reason the feminist movement appears to have waned is that it has been so wildly successful. Feminism has transitioned from being a movement to being the prevailing mind-set of the masses. Virtually every woman is a feminist to one degree or another.[68]

They also noted:

> According to the Bible, maleness and femaleness are essential, not peripheral, to our personhood. Sadly, in an attempt to promote the equality of men and women, our culture has depreciated the unique significance of who God created us to be. As a result, we now have a whole generation that has little if any sense of the beauty, value, and meaning of their manhood or womanhood.[69]

5. Have you been influenced by the dogma of the feminist movement. If so, in what area?

6. Can you give an example of when modern feminism has swayed your thinking regarding your husband, if you have one, or other men in your life?

Man and woman—both created in God's image—alike yet different—flawed by sin—yet designed to showcase God's redemptive plan—the Bridegroom and the Church.

FIXER UPPER

As you examined the temptation of Eve in the garden, did you notice Satan's tactic in undermining God by questioning His goodness and veracity? John Piper and Wayne Grudem bring up another interesting point concerning his tactic in approaching Eve rather than Adam:

We think that Satan's main target was not Eve's peculiar gullibility (if she had one), but rather Adam's headship as the one ordained by God to be responsible for the life of the garden. Satan's subtlety is that he knew the created order God had ordained for the good of the family, and he deliberately defied it by ignoring the man and taking up his dealings with the woman. Satan put her in the position of spokesman, leader, and defender. At that moment both the man and the woman slipped from their innocence and let themselves be drawn into a pattern of relating that to this day has proved destructive.[70]

Do you recognize Satan as a very real enemy? Can you think of a time when you were tempted to doubt God's good intentions toward you? Do you live your life in accordance to His purposes?

DAY THREE

Today, our focus shifts to marriage. The first mention of marriage is found in the Genesis narrative in Chapter 2. God was very specific in His design for marriage, for it established the framework through which God would accomplish his purpose for mankind. Also in His timing, it would mirror God's redemptive plan for Christ and the church.

In Genesis 2:18-20, we find the account of Adam naming all the animals that God had created. In the midst of this process, Adam realized that there was not a helper suitable for him. Of course, this did not take God by surprise for he had already formulated His plan for marriage.

1. Relate what you find in Genesis 2:18 concerning God's solution to Adam's problem.

God thus fashioned Eve, and Adam responded in an enthusiastic manner. And God's plan began to unfold for marriage.

2. Read Genesis 2:24. What three elements did God incorporate in His design for marriage?

This concept of God's design for marriage is skillfully explained in the *Women's Evangelical Commentary of the Old Testament:*

> The fact that the man is said to leave his father and mother indicates that a new unit is forming. Of course, there will still be family ties and responsibilities, but essentially by marriage the man is stepping out to form with his wife a new loyalty that is unbreakable and complete in itself. Because of this intimate bond between a husband and wife, that relationship even supersedes what he has had with his parents. Husband and wife become one, bound in a relationship closer than any other and culminating in the physical union of their two bodies. Family ties still hold, but the loyalty between a man and his wife is primary. The union is absolutely monogamous and exclusive as well as permanent.[71]

3. Examine these passages and record their significance in light of Genesis 2:24. Make note of who is speaking in each.

Matthew 19:3-6

Mark 10:2-9

Ephesians 5:31

The language in Genesis 2:24, especially the verbs *leave* and *join*, indicate that marriage is presented as a covenant relationship even though the word is not actually used in this passage. A study of Scripture reveals that God is a covenant-making and covenant-keeping God so it stands to reason that He would design the covenant dimension within marriage.

Evan Lenow lists some pertinent characteristics about a covenant:

> While there are many opinions on what characteristics make up a covenant, there are at least four that most scholars agree are essential. These are an intimate relationship, a public oath, coordinating sign(s), and perpetual obligations.[72]

4. Can you name a corresponding element of marriage to the four characteristics mentioned in the above quote?

In our culture, however, many adults consider marriage more like a contract that is sustained only when all parties are happy and satisfied. This mindset lends itself to the option of divorce which does not coincide with the permanence ascribed to covenant marriage in Scripture.

5. What changes have you noticed in our culture about attitudes regarding marriage?

As I have been writing this study on the roles of men and women and marriage, I couldn't help but wish that my son, Evan, could have written it. After all, he has been teaching classes for ten years on these topics at Southwestern Baptist Theological Seminary where he is an Associate Professor of Ethics. One side benefit for me is that he frequently updates me on what is transpiring in culture that we all need to be aware of. One of the biggest concerns today is the assault on marriage. So, I would like to share some quotes from a recent article that Evan wrote entitled "The New Marriage Battleground: Polygamy, Polyamory, and Open Marriage." The quotes are lengthy, but I feel that Christians must be informed if the church is going to battle this onslaught against Biblical marriage.

Until the last couple of years, laws in the United States only recognized marriage to be between one man and one woman. The 2015 Supreme Court decision in *Obergefell v. Hodges* opened the door to same-sex marriage. Now we see a push for different types of marriage that infringe upon monogamy.

Polygamy is a marriage arrangement where one individual is married to multiple partners. Historically this is primarily a man married to multiple women. This form of marriage is the one most clearly set up for legalization through the *Obergefell* decision.

Polyamory literally means "many loves" and describes "consensually non-monogamous relationships [where] there is an open agreement that one, both, or all individuals involved in a romantic relationship may also have other sexual and/or romantic partners." Polyamory differs from polygamy because all partners can be in multiple marriage-like relationships.

Open marriage is the third alternative in the marriage battleground. This arrangement involves couples in the marriage being open to romantic, sexual relationships outside the context of their own marriage. . . Proponents of open marriage argue that as long as both spouses are in agreement with the arrangement then it does not break the fidelity of the marriage bond.

The time frame for normalization of these alternative marriages may have accelerated in recent months as a series of articles have been published touting the advantages of various forms of multiple marriage. It is important for us to understand what these are and to critique them from a biblical perspective.

If Scripture depicts God's design for marriage to be monogamous, and if any departure from monogamous marriage is equated with adultery, then the various alternative marriage arrangements—polygamy, polyamory, and open marriage—are all forms of adultery that are subject to the judgment of God. Therefore, Christians should not endorse these forms of "marriage," nor should they tolerate them in their midst.[73]

In the era of political correctness and live and let live, our stand for biblical marriage may be criticized and ridiculed. Yet, it will be worth the cost to stand for righteousness. God designed marriage to His specifications, and while culture's perspective may evolve, His truth never changes.

FIXER UPPER

Years ago, one of my friends decided to divorce her husband. She did not tell me herself, but I heard it through the grapevine. I felt the Lord was leading me to take her to dinner to talk about it, but, quite frankly, I was reluctant to do it. After all, I argued with the Lord, she hadn't even told me about her plan. But, I was obedient, and we met for dinner. As we talked, she told me of her dissatisfaction—her chief complaint was that her husband did not communicate with her. As gently as possible, I related God's plan for marriage. When I finished, she asked, "Is that a Baptist thing?" I replied, "No, it's a Bible thing." I wish I could tell you that she changed her mind, but she did divorce her husband. We are not responsible for the results, but we need to know the truth so that we can share it when the Lord asks us to speak up.

Now I would like to ask you a question. Do you feel competent to share biblical truth regarding God's design for marriage? If not, what will you do to become equipped?

So much is happening in the arena of marriage, but we can be light in a dark world!

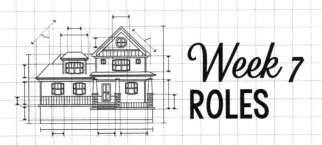

DAY FOUR

God perfectly outlined His plan for marriage in Genesis 2:24, as we learned in our study yesterday. We also observed that Jesus quoted that passage as He responded to the Pharisees regarding divorce and added, "So they are no longer two, but one flesh. What therefore God has joined together, let no man separate" (Matthew 19:6). With these powerful verses in mind, today we will search some key passages from the New Testament to glean some insight into how to practically live out God's instructions in your own marriage. I realize that you may not be married, but I hope that you won't be tempted to skip over this day's study. Knowing God's Truth to share with the people in your life is priceless.

Let's begin with the quintessential passage from Ephesians.

1. Read Ephesians 5:22-33. Outline what the Scripture relates concerning wives.

In this passage, we see the term submission outlined and explained. But through the centuries, women have frequently been resistant to the concept—remember the alienation between men and women as a result of mankind's fall into sin. John Piper and Wayne Grudem define submission in the following quote:

> Submission refers to a wife's divine calling to honor and affirm her husband's leadership and help carry it through according to her gifts. It is not an absolute surrender of her will. Rather, we speak of her *disposition* to yield to her husband's guidance and her *inclination* to follow his leadership. Christ is her absolute authority, not the husband. She submits "out of reverence for Christ" (Ephesians 5:21). The supreme authority of Christ qualifies the authority of her husband. She should never follow her husband into sin. Nevertheless, even when she may have to stand with Christ against the sinful will of her husband (e.g., 1 Peter 3:1, where she does not yield to her husband's unbelief), she can still have a *spirit* of submission—a *disposition* to yield.[74]

2. From the Ephesians passage, notate the instructions given regarding husbands.

Wow! Husbands have a huge assignment—to love their wives as Christ loves the church. Warren Wiersbe gives some practical application to the husbands' assignment in this quote:

> If the husband makes Christ's love for the church the pattern for loving his wife, then he will love her *sacrificially* (Eph. 5:25). Christ gave Himself for the church; so the husband, in love, gives himself for his wife. . . If a husband is submitted to Christ and filled with the Spirit, his sacrificial love will willingly pay a price that she might be able to serve Christ in the home and glorify Him.
>
> The husband's love will also be a *sanctifying* love (Eph. 5:26-27). The word sanctify means "to set apart." In the marriage ceremony, the husband is set apart to belong to the wife, and the wife is set apart to belong to the husband. Any interference with this God-given arrangement is sin. . . The love of the husband for his wife ought to be cleansing her (and him) so that both are becoming more like Christ.
>
> The husband's love for his wife should be sacrificial and sanctifying, but it should also be *satisfying* (Eph. 5:28-30). In the marriage relationship, the husband and wife become "one flesh." Therefore, whatever each does to the other, he does to himself or herself. . . Just as love is the circulatory system to the body of Christ (Eph. 4:16), so love is the nourishment of the home.[75]

3. How does the Apostle Paul correlate the comparison of the marriage relationship and Christ and the church?

Paul calls this comparison a mystery, yet it was within the heart of God before the foundation of the earth. It was a mystery kept hidden until God revealed His redemptive plan. And godly marriage remains a beautiful picture of Christ and the church.

4. What final encouragement does Paul give husbands and wives in Ephesians 5:33?

Love and respect are key elements in a marriage. Emerson Eggerichs speaks candidly about this teaching in his practical book, *Love and Respect*:

> The husband *must* love his wife as he loves himself, and the wife *must* respect her husband. Could it be any clearer than that? Paul isn't making suggestions; he is issuing commands from God himself. In addition, the Greek word Paul uses for love in this verse is *agape*, meaning unconditional love. And the wording of the rest of the passage strongly suggests that the husband should receive unconditional respect. Christian spouses should not read this verse to say, "Husbands, love your wives unconditionally, and wives, respect your husbands only if they have earned and deserve it."[76]

Showing love and respect within marriage is not an option according to Scripture. Neither should it be based on merit. It is God's plan, plain and simple. While the concept is simple, the actual implementation can be challenging to all of us—but we have a Helper, the indwelling Holy Spirit. He makes what seems unattainable possible.

Now we will take a few moments to observe what the Apostle Peter has to say about submission and unconditional love.

5. Read 1 Peter 3:1-7. What extra dimension does Peter add to the consideration of submission? (vs. 1-2)

6. According to Peter, what should a woman's adornment consist of? How would you define it?

7. What would be the consequence of a man failing to live with his wife in a loving way?

We have looked at God's instructions for husband and wives—submission and love. At times we might resist, yet we have a lovely example within the Godhead from which we can gain inspiration. Wayne Grudem provides us with this timely reminder:

> *The idea of headship and submission never began!* It has *always existed* in the eternal nature of God Himself. And in the most basic of all authority relationships, authority is not based on gifts or ability; it is just there. . . . [The relationship between the Father, Son, and Holy Spirit] is one of leadership and authority on the one hand and voluntary, willing, joyful submission to that authority on the other hand. We can learn from this that submission to a rightful authority is a noble virtue. It is a privilege. It is something good and desirable. It is the virtue that has been demonstrated by the eternal Son of God *forever.* It is His glory, the glory of the Son as He relates to His Father.[77]

Jesus is our example. Let's live it out.

FIXER UPPER

You probably remember Elisabeth Elliott as a great woman of the faith. Her husband, Jim Elliott, was martyred by the Auca Indians in Ecuador as he attempted to take them the Gospel. She later followed his lead and took the message of Jesus to the same Indians that had taken his life. Over the years, she wrote several books and spoke around the world. She was married three times, having been widowed twice. I couldn't help but smile at her comment regarding Ephesians 5:22 which reads, "Wives, submit to your own husbands as to the Lord." (ESV)

Many are the discussions I've heard on this one, almost all of them directed to what it "can't possibly mean," rather than to the plain word of the Lord. The statement is simple. Not easy for women like me, but *simple*, that is, I understand it only too well. As Mark Twain said, "I have far more trouble with the things I do understand in the Bible than things I don't understand.[78]

How are you doing with the assignment of submission? Ask the Lord to give you insight. Devise a plan to make any corrections necessary.

Week 7
ROLES

DAY FIVE

This week we have considered God's creation of man and woman, their God-ordained roles in the home, and the challenging responsibility to submit and to love. Also, we looked at the details of the Fall to understand how sin created the battle of the sexes. Down through the ages, there has been conflict between men and women culminating with what we pondered regarding the Women's Lib movement in our study. Mary Kassian and Nancy Leigh DeMoss give some interesting insight into the intermingling of feminism and the church:

> Feminism encompasses much more than the cultural phenomenon of the women's rights movement. It's much more than women having the right to vote, the right to pursue a career, or the right to an abortion. It's much more than the idea that women should be valued and afforded dignity and respect. It's much more than insisting on "fairness" in how the sexes are treated. Feminism is a distinct worldview with its own ideologies, values, and ways of thinking.
>
> Can feminism be embraced along with our Christian faith? Absolutely not. Why not? Because it introduces a subtle (and sometimes not-so-subtle) distortion into the way we approach gender and male-female relationships. It contains truth, but it also contains some powerful and destructive lies. And in so doing, it strikes at the very image of God and at an important earthly picture He chose to display the redemptive story. At its core, feminist philosophy is antithetical to the gospel.[79]

And, as the thinking of the secular society concerning the roles of men and women has altered in the last fifty years, the assessment of the roles within the evangelical church has also come into question. Today, we will research the two schools of thought regarding the roles of men and women in the church.

1. List any changes that you have seen transpire within the church regarding the roles of men and women during your lifetime.

The two views regarding gender and how it should affect both marriage and the church are Complementarian and Egalitarian. Alexander Strauch clearly defines these views in his book, *Equal Yet Different*. In the evangelical church, you will find proponents of both views. Hopefully, the explanation of these views by Strauch will explain what could possibly be unfamiliar terminology to you.

The Complementarian View

The complementarian view teaches that God created men and women as equals with different gender-defined roles. . . . According to this viewpoint, God created men and women equally in His divine image. Men and women are fully equal in personhood, dignity and worth (Genesis 1:26-28).

According to the complementarian viewpoint, it is equally true that God created men and women to be different and to fulfill distinct gender roles. God designed the man to be husband, father, provider, protector. He is to be head of the family and to lead the church family. God designed the woman to be wife, mother, nurturer. She is to actively help and submit to the man's leadership. God designed these differences at creation.

Adherents of the complementarian view believe that it best represents the plain, literal, straightforward teaching of the Bible on gender. Furthermore, role differences are clearly and repeatedly taught and practiced by Jesus Christ and His apostles.

The Egalitarian View (Evangelical Feminist View)

Evangelical feminists teach that God created men and women equally to bear the divine image. Furthermore, they conclude that true equality requires equal ministry opportunities for both sexes. They believe that the submission of the woman in marriage and womanly restrictions in Christian ministry are inconsistent with the true picture of biblical equality. They consider the equal-yet-different doctrine taught by complementarians to be a contradiction in terms.

According to the evangelical feminist view, true biblical equality assures that both men and women are full and equal partners in life. The concept of mutual submission and responsibility determines the relationship between men and women in both marriage and the church. Women and men are free to exercise in the church any and all gifts they possess. Men hold no unique, leadership-authority role solely because of their gender. Leadership and teaching in the church is to be determined by spiritual gift and ability, not gender.[80]

So, we are faced with two contradictory points of view. The Complementarians believe that authority and leadership in the church is delegated by God to men while the Egalitarians hold that it is open to both males and females. How will we determine the truth?

The best strategy is to proceed straight to the Word to ascertain what it has to say. We will not have time to do an extensive study but we will look at some key passages.

2. Read Luke 6:12-16. What did you discover about Jesus' choice of His disciples? How do you know that He took great care in making this decision?

Some would declare that Jesus' choice of only male disciples was based on the culture of the day rather than on a God-ordained choice. Women had little status in the culture, were frequently mistreated, and were not in positions of authority.

3. From your knowledge of the ministry of Jesus, give an example of his treatment of women. Did He reflect the culture of the day?

4. How did Jesus interact with the authority figures of His day, such as the scribes and the Pharisees? Was He concerned with their opinions? Could you see Him compromising to meet their expectations?

5. What did the Apostle Paul instruct Timothy concerning women in 1 Timothy 2:11-15? What reasoning did he give?

Paul has been accused of allowing his bachelor bias to slip into the passage we just read. However, we must remember that this passage is the inspired Word of God and correlates to the other scriptures that we have studied this week on the roles of men and women. Paul was sharing a divine mandate. His use of the words, teaching and authority, point to the position of pastor or elder. Paul was not prohibiting women from teaching for there are many areas where women can teach within the church—such as Women's Ministry! John Piper and Wayne Grudem put forth the complementarian point of view in this quote:

> We would say that the teaching inappropriate for a woman is the teaching of men in settings
> or ways that dishonor the calling of men to bear the primary responsibility for teaching and
> leadership. This primary responsibility is to be carried out by the pastors or elders. Therefore
> we think it is God's will that only men bear the responsibility for this office.[81]

In light of the prevailing thought in our culture today regarding equality, it is not surprising that some would take issue with God's design for man and woman. God is the authority who made that decision and while secular society would argue against it, His ruling stands.

But I want you to understand that Christ is the head of every man, and the man is
the head of a woman, and God is the head of Christ.
1 Corinthians 11:3

Jesus, Our Example!

‖‖‖

We have only scratched the surface of this challenging study. As you have surmised, the battle of the sexes, which had its origin at the Fall, has crept into the life of the church, as well. What can we do to make a difference in our world that seems to have turned upside down? I would like to share this challenge from Mary Kassian with you. Won't you pray about how you could make a difference in our culture?

I believe the time is ripe for a new movement—a seismic holy quake of countercultural men and women who dare to take God at His Word—men and women whose hearts are broken over the gender confusion and spiritual/emotional/relational carnage of our day, and who have the courage to believe and delight in God's plan for male and female.[82]

‖‖‖

Week 8
FORGIVENESS

"...forgiving one another, just as God through Christ has forgiven you."
Ephesians 4:32, NLT

Jesus gave us the command to forgive others as He has forgiven us. Then He gave us a model to follow on the cross. Even when He was being killed by an angry mob, Jesus prayed, 'Father, forgive them; for they do not know what they are doing' (Luke 23:34). Following Jesus' example, we need to forgive others without conditions. When we release others, we can know the cleansing and forgiving work of God in our lives as well. [83]

—Oscar W. Thompson, Jr.

You found the one! The perfect property! You can see the end result in your mind. But first, much work has to be done. Talk about the need for a makeover? This one checks all of the boxes. How in the world are you ever going to get there? It is time to assess the damage. It is time to go <u>inside</u> and scour over the place. What needs to be ripped out and tossed? What needs to be replaced?

This sounds like a reasonable starting place for your latest fixer-upper project, doesn't it? A legitimate checklist to get things started.

The same is true in the area of forgiveness.

Before we can fix it all up...that broken relationship, hurting marriage, strained friendship...we must first look inside. We need to open the door to our heart and honestly and thoroughly scour over the mess. We need the spotlight of the Holy Spirit to shine in every corner and crevice as to not miss a single problem.

DAY ONE

To begin this week, I want to invite you into my own personal "fixer-upper" in the area of forgiveness. I will share with you my "demo day" and we will journey together through the remainder of the week to see what God's Word teaches us about forgiveness.

I have not attained all I need to learn in the area of forgiveness, but God has graciously and powerfully taught me a great deal about the importance and necessity to forgive. Not only to forgive, but to forgive *"just as God through Christ has forgiven you"* (Ephesians 4:32, NLT).

My fixer-upper story comes by way of my marriage. At the time of this writing, my husband and I have been married for 16 years. The first several years of our marriage were drenched in deep pain, betrayal, neglect and distrust. As you can imagine, this led to a very strained and broken relationship, not in line with God's creative design for husband and wife. I began to feel justified in my negative feelings toward my husband. "He created this." "This is his fault." "I do not deserve this." "How could I have gotten myself into such a mess?" These are some of the thoughts with which the enemy began to assault my mind.

For me, a root of bitterness, as a result of unforgiveness, grew deeper and deeper because I allowed the devil to infiltrate my mind and thoughts. Donna Gaines often reminds us, "Feelings are not truth." In my turmoil, I began basing my attitude and actions on feelings rather than God's truth. Before I continue, let's take a look at Scripture concerning our minds.

1. As you read these verses, jot down your thoughts as it relates to your mind. If we are not walking in obedience to these truths, how can we be affected in the area of forgiveness?

   Philippians 4:8

   Proverbs 4:23

   Ephesians 4:22-23

   Proverbs 3:5

   2 Corinthians 10:5

For me, the first step in this process was a realization that I had allowed my mind to be taken captive to my own line of reasoning rather than the truth of God's Word. I had begun to make an idol of all that I saw to be wrong in my marriage.

In his book, *The Pursuit of God*, A.W. Tozer writes about God calling Abraham to sacrifice his son, Isaac. He says this of the relationship.

> From the moment he first stooped to take the tiny form awkwardly in his arms, he was an eager love slave of his son. God went out of His way to comment on the strength of this affection. And it is not hard to understand. The baby represented everything sacred to his father's heart: the promises of God, the covenants, the hopes of the years and the long messianic dream. As he watched him grow from babyhood to young manhood, the heart of the old man was knit closer and closer with the life of his son, till at last the relationship bordered upon the perilous. It was then that God stepped in to save both father and son from the consequences of an uncleansed love.

> Tozer goes on to say that it was as if God said to Abraham, I never intended that you should actually slay the lad. I only wanted to remove him from the temple of your heart that I might reign unchallenged there. [84]

God began to reveal the condition of my heart, showing me I had made gods out of my thoughts and disappointments. My mind was dwelling on all I wanted to see changed in my husband rather than on the condition of my own heart. I had grown bitter. I had not forgiven. Not as Christ had forgiven me. With my mouth, I said I had forgiven. With my heart, I had not.

This was the beginning of a transformation. The remodel was underway. God was chiseling away those old cabinets and drawers of my heart where I had stored anger and resentment. He was knocking out old darkened windows that blinded my eyes to His perfect truth. He was ripping up the old stinky carpet that lined my heart, lies that soaked in and settled like mold and mildew. It was demo day!

I remember the moment. Unlike the hard throw of a cold, metal hammer, God gently prodded my heart to reach out to my husband. He gently called me to obey Him, to extend the hand of grace and forgiveness…real forgiveness…and allow Him to begin the process of healing and restoration for which I had desperately prayed.

So, I did it. I obeyed. I won't say that I did it without hesitation and reluctance. I knew I was at a crossroads. I had a choice to make. Would I sit in that old decrepit, run down house of a stony and stubborn heart? Or would I be willing to endure the mess of a remodel?

I am happy to report the big reveal was worth it! Just like a home renovation project, it isn't perfect. Fixer-uppers are ongoing projects. There are always things that pop up that need a touch up or a tweak here and there. Our lives are much the same. We will not be complete until we stand before Him face to face, but until then, are you willing to let Him in to carefully inspect your heart and get this renovation underway?

2. Grab your Bible. Read Psalm 139:23, Psalm 51:10, and Ephesians 5:10-11. Then use them as a basis to write a prayer.

3. As you pray, ask God to reveal any area of unforgiveness in your heart. If you are struggling to forgive someone, write it out in the space below.

Tell the Lord of your hurt and pain. Confess your sin if you feel anger, bitterness or hate. Ask Him to forgive you and then ask Him to help you begin the process of forgiveness. Consider sharing this with a trusted friend this week and ask her to pray for you as you allow God to remodel and renovate your heart. And then, sit back and watch Him work!

DAY TWO

Now that we have surveyed the damage and cleaned out the mess, let's begin with a new foundation. Let us begin from the ground up and make sure we have a sure footing on which to build. What better blueprint than God's Word!

1. Read these verses and record what God says about forgiveness.

    Colossians 3:13

    Luke 17:3-4

    Ephesians 4:32

    Mark 11:25

2. How do these truths differ from our natural response? Our society? What lies does the enemy attack us with to combat these truths from God's Word?

3. After reading through the previous verses, which of these is most difficult for you? Why?

Rick Warren says, "Real forgiveness is unconditional. There's no attachment to it. You don't earn it. You don't deserve it. You don't bargain for it. Forgiveness is not based on a promise to never do it again. You offer it to somebody whether they ask for it or not." [85]

So, where do we begin? The scriptures we've looked at today have commanded us to forgive. Let us look closely at Jesus Christ and the forgiveness He has lavished upon us so that we, in turn, can obey His commands to forgive. The Bible tells us in Acts 16:31 that to be saved, we must believe in the Lord Jesus. God has made receiving His forgiveness quite simple. He calls us to repent of, to turn away from, our sin, and to believe (Acts 3:19, Acts 20:21, 2 Corinthians 7:10, Acts 2:38, Romans 10:13).

In order to forgive according to God's Word, we must understand, as best we can, how God has forgiven us. Whether you've been a Christian for a few days or several years, take a few moments to settle into these verses and be reminded of the unfathomable gift of God's forgiveness.

4. What do the following verses teach us about God's forgiveness? Which resonates most powerfully with you?

    Psalm 103:10-12

    Colossians 1:13, 22

    Exodus 34:5-7

    Micah 7:18-19

    Hebrews 10:17

5. How can we open ourselves to and accept God's forgiveness?

   1 John 1:9

   Psalm 32:3, 5

   Luke 18:9-14

   Psalm 86:5

David said it best in Psalm 32:1 when he declared, *"Oh, what joy for those whose disobedience is forgiven, whose sin is put out of sight!"* (NLT)

Repeat this verse aloud. Let the words echo through your mind. Contemplate God's forgiveness for <u>your</u> sin.

6. Take a few moments to write out your thoughts on the forgiveness of God and thank Him for what He has done.

Commit today to forgive as He forgives. In *Reclaiming Surrendered Ground*, Jim Logan says,

God is not asking me to feel something, but to do something. When God told Moses to stretch out his staff over the Red Sea, he could have doubted, even being resentful that God had put him in this predicament—the approaching Egyptian army pinning him against the sea and his people, unarmed, tired from the journey, some of them complaining. Moses could have complained and refused. Instead, he did as God commanded, because it was God who asked and because Moses knew who God was. Faith demands a warrant, a grounds for belief. A warrant is a legal document on which an action is based. God's Word, His promise to act, was the warrant for Moses' faith. We know he had faith because of his actions. That's the way it is with forgiveness. We can respond with forgiveness even when our feelings say no, for God's Word commands us and promises His blessings to those who do forgive. [86]

DAY THREE

This week we have learned that forgiveness is a command given to us by God. As with all commands in Scripture, we have a choice to make. So, what if we choose to <u>not</u> forgive? As Vicki Kraft explains,

> Life offers us plenty of opportunities to feel unforgiving. The trouble is, lack of forgiveness does more damage to us than to the offender. When we don't forgive, we grow hardened, untrusting, sour, and bitter. We become vengeful. We want the person who wronged us to suffer. Those negative feelings war against the love and compassion that should characterize us as Christians, and we hinder our own spiritual growth. [87]

We learned from Ephesians 4:32 earlier this week to forgive as Christ forgives. The previous verse begins by telling us to *get rid of all bitterness* (Ephesians 4:31, NLT). We must first rid ourselves of *all types of evil behavior,* which includes bitterness.

1. Read Hebrews 12:15 to see the effect of a bitter heart. Have you experienced this in your life? In the life of your family?

This verse cautions us against a root of bitterness taking hold in our hearts. As the Scripture tells us, it not only troubles us but corrupts many.

Think about the root system of a tree. Tree roots are very strong — even new roots. Because they are driven toward water and nutrients, tree roots constantly extend themselves as they search.

Just as the large tree in the neighbor's yard may have an impact on your yard or foundation, so can the roots of bitterness in your own heart. These roots, however small they may be, will continue to go deeper and deeper and will begin to interfere in other areas. We cannot allow bitterness to take any root at all.

My research on root-related damage led me to these findings:

> One way to address the issue is to build a root barrier. In order to do so, you may have to dig all the way down to the base of your home's foundation. You can cut away roots that are approaching your foundation while you're digging for the barrier. The process can be a hassle, but it's better than merely trusting that your home will be left undamaged by weather cycles and root growth…Another way to prevent tree roots from causing damage is to reconsider your plans for tree planting in the area around your home. [88]

2. As you consider these findings, compare the damage of the root of bitterness and how it can be dealt with and avoided in your life.

3. Our hearts will be rooted in something. Read these verses to see God's intention for where our deep roots should lie.

Jeremiah 17:7-8

Ephesians 3:17-19

Colossians 2:6-7

Proverbs 12:3

4. Evaluate your own root system. Conduct a soil analysis on your heart. Has a root of bitterness taken hold in your heart as a result of unforgiveness? Use the diagram below to identify those roots that need to be dealt with and ask the Lord to begin the process of removal.

Kraft also observes,

> If we won't forgive, bitterness will become firmly entrenched in our characters. It will make us cynical, unable to trust, and unable to maintain close relationships. Just as in Jesus' parable of the unforgiving servant who was sent to the torturers, our own bitterness will torture us for a lifetime. On the other hand, forgiveness will free us to go on in peace, unhindered in our enjoyment of the Lord. Let's forgive. [89]

Forgiveness is one of the marks of a true believer. I want others to look at my life and say, "How in the world can she possibly forgive _____?" I hope to share what Jesus has done for me and that real freedom is found in offering forgiveness God's way.

Deuteronomy 28:2 tells us we will experience the blessings of God if we obey Him. The next couple days of our study will look closely at the blessings of forgiveness and a powerful example of this truth.

DAY FOUR

Today, we will look at Psalm 32 (TLB) and see the blessings of forgiveness. Read through the text below and meditate on the nature and character of God as you consider His forgiveness. Jot down your thoughts in the margin as you read.

Psalm 32

What happiness for those whose guilt has been forgiven! What joys when sins are covered over! What relief for those who have confessed their sins and God has cleared their record. There was a time when I wouldn't admit what a sinner I was. But my dishonesty made me miserable and filled my days with frustration. All day and all night your hand was heavy on me. My strength evaporated like water on a sunny day until I finally admitted all my sins to you and stopped trying to hide them. I said to myself, "I will confess them to the Lord." And you forgave me! All my guilt is gone. Now I say that each believer should confess his sins to God when he is aware of them, while there is time to be forgiven. Judgment will not touch him if he does. You are my hiding place from every storm of life; you even keep me from getting into trouble! You surround me with songs of victory. I will instruct you (says the Lord) and guide you along the best pathway for your life; I will advise you and watch your progress. Don't be like a senseless horse or mule that has to have a bit in its mouth to keep it in line. Many sorrows come to the wicked, but abiding love surrounds those who trust in the Lord. So rejoice in him, all those who are his, and shout for joy, all those who try to obey him.

1. Read Exodus 34:6-7. What do you see here about God's nature in relation to forgiveness?

2. Can you reflect back on a time when God was slow to anger, showing you His compassion and mercy?

God <u>wants</u> to forgive us. He desires that we, as His children, experience joy. Are you experiencing guilt as a result of unconfessed sin? Psalm 32:1-2 tells us that we will experience joy when our record is cleared of guilt. Only Jesus Christ can declare, "Not guilty!" This comes through confessing sin and receiving the forgiveness of our Lord and Savior Jesus Christ. As *The Life Application Study Bible* says, "To confess our sin is to agree with God, acknowledging that He is right to declare what we have done as sinful and that we are wrong to desire or to do it. It means affirming our intention of forsaking that sin in order to follow God more faithfully."[90] Paul reiterated in Romans 4:7-8 the words from this Psalm, declaring that our disobedience is forgiven and our sin is put out of sight! That is some good news!

Martin Luther said, "Sin has but two places where it may be; either it may be with you, so that it lies upon your neck, or upon Christ, the Lamb of God. If now it lies upon your neck, you are lost; if, however, it lies upon Christ, you are free and will be saved."[91]

3. Let us consider the beauty and depth of God's forgiveness. When David declares in Psalm 32 that our "disobedience is forgiven" and our "sin is put out of sight," what does this mean?

Our sin is covered and not counted. It is out of sight and not charged to our account. Steven Cole explains, "God will never bring up our sins as a matter of judgment between Him and us. If we're in Christ, our sins are covered by His blood!"[92]

4. What does this truth speak to your heart? How does this play out in the life of a believer?

5a. What did David experience when he refused to confess his sin (v. 3, 4)?

5b. Have you experienced similar circumstances as a result of unconfessed sin?

Verse 6 begins with "therefore," leading us to believe the following verses are a consequence of receiving God's forgiveness as a result of confessing sin.

6.   Read Psalm 32:6-8. What blessings do we receive as forgiven children of God?

God is our refuge. He is compassionate and merciful. He is filled with unfailing love and faithfulness. He wants to lavish His love on us from generation to generation. This is our God. Yes, He deals with our sin and takes it seriously. Yes, He disciplines us and it can be heavy. But, oh how He loves us!

Imagine a whiteboard. Picture every single sin written out one by one. Every thought. Every deed. Every word. All the hidden things that only you know. Think of the weight, the embarrassment, the guilt, the shame. Now, picture a Savior, a Redeemer, the Lover of your soul. Imagine Him walking in and looking you in the eye. Rather than chastise and condemn, He gently passes by and picks up the eraser. His nail pierced hand reaches up and begins to erase. Every thought. Every deed. Every word.

"Unfailing love surrounds those who trust the Lord. So rejoice in the LORD and be glad, all you who obey Him! Shout for joy, all you whose hearts are pure!" (Psalm 32:10b-11, NLT)

As we walk in obedience to the Lord by confessing our sin, He lavishly pours out His forgiveness on us. This leads to immeasurable joy! Our hearts are pure and clean and it should cause us, like David, to shout for joy and be glad. Do others see this joy in you?

John Calvin sums it up this way: "David here teaches us that the happiness of men consists only in the free forgiveness of sins, for nothing can be more terrible than to have God for our enemy; nor can He be gracious to us in any other way than by pardoning our transgressions."[93]

Close out your time today by confessing any sin that comes to mind. Allow Him to cleanse and purify your heart right now. Reread Psalm 32 once more to be reminded of the blessings of forgiveness. Thank Him and praise Him for the gift of His forgiveness.

DAY FIVE

As I sit down to pen these words for this last day, my heart is overflowing. On this day in 1982, I accepted Jesus Christ as my personal Lord and Savior. My God is not a God of coincidence. He is a God of perfect timing. He orchestrates all things according to His plan and purpose. Before the foundation of the world, He knew I would sit in this café on this day and wrap up a week of study on forgiveness. What better way to consider forgiveness than to reflect back on the most important decision of my entire life!

I recently watched a marriage series by Tim Kimmel, *Grace Based Marriage*. One of the most poignant statements was, "Revisit the cross daily."[94] As he encouraged us to view our spouse through a grace based lens, he pointed us back to the cross. That statement burned in my heart and still, to this day, replays in my mind almost daily.

How could I possibly withhold forgiveness as I look at Calvary?

1. Read one of the gospel accounts of the crucifixion (Matthew 27:27-56; Mark 15:16-41; Luke 23:26-49; John 19:17-37) and be reminded of the agony of the cross. Jesus forgave you and me and those that nailed his feet and hands to the tree. He wiped our slate clean before we even entered the world. Don't skim over it. Don't breeze through the text due to its familiarity. Take time today to revisit the cross.

One of the most beautiful demonstrations of forgiveness is in Genesis where we see the account of Joseph and his brothers. (Genesis 37 tells of Joseph being sold into slavery by his brothers. Chapters 39 and 40 give account of Joseph's hardship and suffering as a result of being sold into slavery.)

Following these most difficult circumstances, Joseph is placed in charge of Egypt (Genesis 41). He rises from prison walls to Pharaoh's palace.

We see God's sovereignty through these chapters of Genesis as God's perfect plan unfolds in the midst of seemingly hopeless circumstances. As Joseph said to his brothers, "You intended to harm me, but God intended it all for good. He brought me to this position so I could save the lives of many people" (Genesis 50:20, NLT).

What brought Joseph to this point of declaring God's goodness and sovereignty? He certainly demonstrated trust in a most powerful way. He also chose to forgive. *The Life Application Study Bible* observes, "Joseph's forgiveness was complete. He demonstrated how God graciously accepts us even though we don't deserve it."[95] Joseph's brothers did not deserve forgiveness, yet he forgave and even took it a step further. Not only did he forgive them, he reassured them and offered to care for them and their families (Genesis 50:15-21).

So, how is this possible? How does this play out in our individual lives and in our homes?

2. Look up the following verses and make note of the principle found in God's Word. Use these to create a "blueprint" for forgiveness in your home.

Ecclesiastes 7:20

Matthew 7:12

Mark 11:25

Romans 12:19

1 Corinthians 13:5b

Matthew 18:21-22

Luke 6:28b

3. Consider these areas of your life. Where does forgiveness need to take place? Has it taken place and how have you seen God bless as a result of obedience?

- Marriage:

- Children:

- Family relationships:

- Friendship:

- Co-worker/Competitor:

- In ministry/service:

Rick Warren notes:

> The Bible says, *"We know that our old life died with Christ on the cross so that our sinful selves would have no power over us and we would not be slaves to sin"* (Romans 6:6 NCV). Don't be a slave any longer to the sin of unforgiveness. Release your grip on the person who hurt you. Do it every day if you have to. No matter how often that painful memory returns, bring it to God, ask for his grace, and then leave your hurt at the cross. Forgiveness is free. But it's not cheap. It cost Jesus Christ his life. [96]

Revisit the cross daily. <u>This</u> is the key to forgiveness.

||||||||||||||||||||||||||||||||||||||||||||||||||||||||||||||||||||||||||||||||||||||||||||||||||||||||||||||||||||||||||||||||||||||||||||||||||||

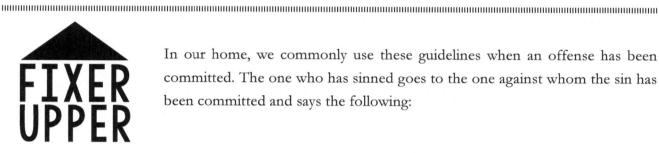

In our home, we commonly use these guidelines when an offense has been committed. The one who has sinned goes to the one against whom the sin has been committed and says the following:

1. I am sorry for _____ (Name the sin specifically).

2. This was wrong because _____ (State how this goes against God's word. It's important to recognize we have disobeyed God's word as we sin against others.)

3. Next time, I will _____ (Offer a commitment to choose wisely next time and name that specifically.)

4. Will you please forgive me?

We emphasize that once sin is confessed, repented of and forgiven, it is done! We do not have to repeatedly ask God for forgiveness for the same sin, so we make sure to practice this within our family. It is finished!

What guidelines do you use in your home to display and practice the art of biblical forgiveness?

||||||||||||||||||||||||||||||||||||||||||||||||||||||||||||||||||||||||||||||||||||||||||||||||||||||||||||||||||||||||||||||||||||||||||||||||||||

Week 9
GRATITUDE

DAY ONE

These things I have spoken to you so that My joy may be in you, and that your joy may be made full.

John 15:11

The key words for our study this week are "gratitude" and "joy." In the biblical sense, gratitude is best described as the natural expression of thanks in response to God's goodness to us. Joy is an attitude of delight rooted and derived in Jesus Christ. Far more than happiness which relies on circumstances, joy is a state of delight and well-being that results from knowing and serving God. Being grateful typically results in joy. As we entrust ourselves into the hands of our Heavenly Father and develop a thankful heart towards Him, the joy of Jesus becomes manifestly evident in our lives.

An attitude of gratitude and the joy of the Lord are often linked together. To illustrate this principle together, we will be looking at a passage in Luke 1:5-56. In this passage we read about two supernatural births. First let's look at the story of Zacharias and Elizabeth, who had been unable to conceive.

1a. Read Luke 1:5-25. What was the angel's message to Zacharias?

1b. What did the angel tell Zacharias about the son that would be born to him and his wife Elizabeth?

1c. How did Zacharias respond to the angel's pronouncement?

1d. What happened to Zacharias because of his unbelief?

In our text, we move from a miraculous birth, to a couple advanced in age, to another miraculous birth conceived in the womb of a virgin. Both pregnancies were announced by the angel Gabriel.

We are introduced to Mary when the angel visited her in Luke 1:26-27. God sovereignly chose her to be the singular instrument to bring forth Messiah into the world. What remarkable grace and privilege was granted to this woman!

We do not know Mary's exact age, but culturally it was customary for girls to be betrothed while they were as young as thirteen years of age. Mary was betrothed to a young man named Joseph. We know very little about him except that he was a carpenter (see Mark 6:3) by trade and described as *a righteous man* (Matthew 1:19). Her betrothal to Joseph was a legal engagement, which generally lasted a full year. It was as binding as a marriage covenant and could only be dissolved by a divorce. During this year the couple lived apart and had no physical relations whatsoever. The year-long engagement demonstrated the fidelity of both partners. During the betrothal of Mary and Joseph the angel appeared to her.

2a. Read Luke 1:26-38. The dialogue between Gabriel and Mary is recorded for us. How did Gabriel greet Mary?

Mary was perplexed by the angel's words and evidently a bit afraid.

2b. What did the angel tell Mary about the Child she would conceive?

Mary struggled to grasp the angel's message about a child since she was a virgin. Gabriel told Mary that her relative Elizabeth was six months pregnant.

2c. What was Mary's response to such a glorious pronouncement?

Mary's response to Gabriel is one worth pondering, especially when compared to Zacharias' reaction to an equally miraculous promise of a child. In the moment, Zacharias' faith faltered in light of his and Elizabeth's advanced age. On the other hand, Mary responded to the angel's pronouncement with the grace, wisdom, and spiritual maturity of a seasoned saint. Mary said, "Behold, the bondslave of the Lord; may it be done to me according to your word" (Luke 1:38).

Filled with unspeakable joy, Mary arose and went to see her relative, Elizabeth. Gabriel had revealed to Mary the miraculous pregnancy of her beloved cousin, who was possibly now in her eighties and had been previously unable to conceive.

3a. Read Luke 1:39-45. What happened to Elizabeth when she heard Mary's greeting?

3b. What did she say to Mary?

Elizabeth does not seem to have had any prior knowledge of Mary's pregnancy. Her knowledge of the impending birth of the Holy Child seems to have come to her by divine revelation as evidenced by the prophecy she uttered when the Holy Spirit suddenly filled her. Surely Elizabeth's response was a faith-builder to Mary.

Certainly every godly woman in Mary's ancestry, going all the way back to Eve, had longed to be the one through whom the Redeemer would come. Mary, a virtually unknown Jewish girl, was granted that privilege.

Mary is given a low profile in the gospel accounts. The Lord Jesus Christ is the central focus of the good news! During Jesus' earthly ministry, one day a woman "in the crowd raised her voice and said to Him, 'Blessed is the womb that bore You, and the breasts at which you nursed.' Jesus gently corrected her and replied, "On the contrary, blessed are those who hear the word of God, and observe it" (Luke 11:27-28). Christ is central to the gospel message.

At Elizabeth's prophetic utterance confirming Gabriel's message, Mary launched into an outpouring of praise and unspeakable joy. Her song has been deemed, "The Magnificat."

4a. Read Luke 1:46-55. What names does Mary use to describe God?

4b. How does Mary view herself?

Mary's offering of praise to the Lord contains twenty-five Old Testament passages. She was a very young woman, but she knew the Word! Traditionally, Jewish boys were trained in the Scriptures while Jewish girls were generally taught homemaking skills. We do not know who had taught Mary but we marvel at her working knowledge of God's Word.

From this extended passage we see two miraculous pregnancies. We sympathize with Zacharias who suffered a momentary lapse of faith when he applied human logic to Gabriel's revelation. We marvel at the faith of Mary, a young Jewish girl, upon hearing she would be the human vessel by which would come the Savior of the world! We are amazed at her obedience. Mary surrendered herself to the will of the Father without knowing all the details. We can't help but rejoice at Elizabeth's miraculous pregnancy. Her baby, who would grow up to be John the Baptist, leapt in her womb when Mary arrived in their home. We marvel at Mary's spiritual maturity. We are stunned by her worship, full of thanksgiving and praise for what God had accomplished in her young life.

The goal for today's study was to inspire and encourage you as you build your household of faith on the firm foundation of Jesus Christ. May we desire to build a life overflowing with gratitude for God's unspeakable gift of the Lord Jesus Christ as our substitute for sin. May we also seek a life overflowing with joy that others might see Jesus in us!

DAY TWO

Today we are studying the word "gratitude." As a mom I began early to teach my sons to be grateful. I wanted them to learn to appreciate the many blessings they were the happy recipient of and appreciate what my husband and I (and others who were investing in their lives) were doing for them. This was in preparation to teach them to be grateful for what God had done for them through the Lord Jesus. 1 Thessalonians 5:18 says, "In everything give thanks; for this is God's will for you in Christ Jesus." Give thanks. Be grateful. This is God's will. Gratitude is a learned response. Grumbling is a natural response lingering in our base nature, the flesh.

Beloved, developing a thankful heart can drastically revolutionize your walk with God. All spiritual disciplines must be diligently practiced in order to demolish the habit patterns held over from our lives prior to conversion. As the mind is renewed by the Word of God, the life is transformed through the Spirit of God.

1a. Look at James 1:17. How are these gifts from above described?

1b. What is the origin of everything we have?

1c. How is God described?

God is a good Father and He gives good gifts, although some of those gifts come by way of sorrow and seasons of sufferings. Often, God's scales measure the merit of His good gifts differently than we do. In response to His grace gifts, the only appropriate response is one of gratitude. Gratefulness is a determined response issuing forth from a conditioned mind focused on Jesus Christ. Don't wait until the middle of your trial to decide on being grateful and trusting in God's character and nature.

2. Read Ephesians 5:18-20. Paul contrasts the control wine exerts over the mind, will, and emotions (which can lead to a lack of judgment resulting in debauchery) with being filled with the Spirit. Therefore instead of being drunk with wine we are to be filled with the Spirit, allowing Him to control and direct our lives. In similar fashion when the Spirit controls our minds, wills, and emotions the fruit of the Spirit is produced in us. What characterizes the lives of Spirit-filled believers?

In Ephesians 5:20, Paul challenges us to give "thanks for all things in the name of our Lord Jesus Christ to God, even the Father." He admonishes us to be thankful in all things because we reside under the watchful eye of our Heavenly Father.

3. Look up Romans 8:31-32. Why, according to this passage, should we trust God wholeheartedly?

The ability to fully trust God in all circumstances is one of the components of developing gratitude in all things.

4a. Read Luke 11:11-13. Jesus uses an outlandish illustration to illustrate the love of God towards His children. What does Luke record of that conversation about our earthly fathers?

4b. What conclusion should we draw about God and His ability to provide?

As we mature in our faith we learn to rest in the sovereignty of God, which allows us to view our circumstances through our Father's eye. We become convinced that nothing can come into our life before it is filtered through the hand and heart of God the Father. Father-filtered faith. It rests in the divine wisdom of God to orchestrate all things for our good and His glory.

Beloved, we can trust God implicitly. We should develop an attitude of gratitude consistently. We should thank God constantly. "Blessed be the Lord, who daily bears our burden, the God who is our salvation" (Psalm 68:19). In Christ, we are tightly held and unconditionally loved by God. The only correct response to love so amazing is a heart overflowing with gratitude.

||||||||||||||||||||||||||||||||||||||||||||||||||||||||||||||||||||||||||||||||||||||||||||||||||||||||||||||||||||||||||||||||||||||||||||||||||||||||||||||

We bring a mind trained in depravity when we believe on the Lord Jesus Christ and receive Him. If we are not diligent to renew our minds with God's Word, we will repeat the sinful habit patterns deeply ingrained in us before conversion. The apostle Paul wrote, "For I know that nothing good dwells in me, that is, in my flesh; for the willing is present in me, but the doing of the good is not. For the good that I want, I do not do, but I practice the very evil that I do not want" (Romans 7:18-19). We must strive to demolish the sinful habit patterns of our lives prior to conversion by renewing our minds with the Word of God and surrendering our wills to the Spirit of God.

||||||||||||||||||||||||||||||||||||||||||||||||||||||||||||||||||||||||||||||||||||||||||||||||||||||||||||||||||||||||||||||||||||||||||||||||||||||||||||||

Week 9
GRATITUDE

DAY THREE

Happiness and joy are vastly different states, especially for the Bible-believing Christian. Happiness is an emotion based on circumstance, while joy is a fruit of the Spirit and is only reserved for believers.

Our study today is on the topic of joy. We will be looking at James 1:1-4. Here is some background that will help us dig deeper in our study on the word "joy." The epistle of James was written by the half-brother of Jesus Christ. James was the first child born of the union of Mary and Joseph after the supernatural birth of Jesus. Their family grew to include brothers, Joses, Judas, Simon (Mark 6:3; Matthew 13:55) and some sisters.

Isn't it interesting that James does not reference his earthly relationship to Jesus in his salutation? In fact, James never even alludes to the familial relationship the men shared during our Lord's earthly visitation. Instead, James opened his letter with his testimony to the saving power of the resurrected Lord of Glory and his choice privilege of being His bond-slave. The earthly ties that had made James and Jesus half-brothers were eclipsed by the heavenly ties that made them joint-heirs in the family of God.

1. Read James 1:2-4. James instructs believers on the proper response to the various trials we will encounter. What is it?

Trials are common to everyone, believers and unbelievers. We live in a broken world which results in broken relationships, broken promises, and broken hearts. Becoming a Christian does not make us immune to hardships and difficult circumstances, but rather gives us access to the power to respond differently than unbelievers. The indwelling Holy Spirit supplies us with the joy of the Lord if we are willing to respond in obedience and appropriate it.

2. According to James 1:3, what is the end result of a proper response to testing?

While no one would seek suffering, when we encounter it we can rest in the knowledge that God is using it to build endurance in our lives. It is worth noting that sin always causes suffering, but not all suffering is the result of sin. God uses suffering to produce spiritual growth and fruitfulness in our lives.

3. Look at our text again. Properly understood, what is the perfect result of endurance?

Rightly understood, God allows us to encounter tests in order to produce endurance, which results in spiritual maturity. Therefore, we can consider it all joy when we encounter various trials.

4a. Read 1 Peter 1:6-8. Peter writes a similar passage to convey a similar truth. According to this passage, what is a proper response to various trials?

4b. How does he describe the proof of a faith that can stand up to testing?

Peter had been an eyewitness to the earthly ministry of Jesus. We can assume his faith had been bolstered, at least in part, by that experience. Peter commends the faith of those who have not seen Him yet believe. "Though you have not seen Him, you love Him, and though you do not see Him now, but believe in Him, you greatly rejoice with joy inexpressible and full of glory, obtaining as the outcome of your faith the salvation of your souls" (1 Peter 1:8-9). Genuine saving faith can endure trials of testing and produce joy in the child of God who trusts Him.

Trials are sent by God or allowed by Him to strengthen our faith and produce spiritual maturity. Temptation to sin is sent by the devil to cause us to stumble. James is quite clear; "God cannot be tempted by evil, and He Himself does not tempt anyone" (James 1:13). God tests our faith to mature it. Satan tempts us with evil in an effort to cause us to stumble into sin, damage our Christian testimony, and impede our forward progress of sanctification in the Lord. As believers we have the spiritual power to overcome the temptations of the world, the flesh, and the devil. "Greater is He who is in [us] than he who is in the world" (1 John 4:4).

We cannot avoid hurt and heartache. We will encounter various trials. That is part and parcel of our broken world. We can, however, avoid falling headlong into the snares of the devil. We can consider it all joy when life grows increasingly difficult by walking by faith in obedience to the Word and dependence on the Spirit of God.

5. Read James 1:12. What is promised to those who persevere under trials?

The love of God, both our love for Him and His love for us, sustains us when we encounter seasons of suffering and trials.

DAY FOUR

For our study on the subject of gratitude, I chose one of the most grateful woman I have ever read about in the New Testament. Her name is Mary Magdalene, and Luke introduces her in his gospel.

1. Read Luke 8:1-3. What do we find out about Mary Magdalene from this passage?

Demons. Seven of them. This dark piece of Mary's past life reveals some of her background, making her rise to prominence among Jesus' followers all the more remarkable. The Scripture offers no particulars about how or when Mary become demon-possessed or her encounter with Jesus Christ when He delivered her. We do know that Jesus revealed Himself to her as Savior and Lord and she responded in repentance and faith. Jesus brought an abrupt end to her savage captivity, restored her right mind, and freed her to follow Him.

After Jesus saved Mary Magdalene, she was brought into the fellowship of His followers. She became part of the privileged group of women who accompanied Jesus and His twelve disciples and was given a front-row seat to the Kingdom of God in action.

Like the others, Mary Magdalene stumbled over Jesus' words about the cross. She couldn't wrap her brain around the crucifixion or the miracle of resurrection when He spoke of it. When the nightmarish events surrounding the crucifixion began in earnest, she was powerless to help and unable to comprehend the events as they unfolded. Nevertheless, throughout the horrifying ordeal Mary Magdalene stayed with Jesus.

Mary Magdalene's presence at the cross is reported by all four Gospel writers. Despite the looming danger and the gruesome brutality of the cross, Mary and the other women stayed. The Scriptures do not record Mary's thoughts or reactions as she endured the heart-wrenching scene playing out before her eyes, but the vicious savagery of the cross was the kind of life-altering trauma that scars the soul for all time.

Matthew writes,

"When it was evening, there came a rich man from Arimathea, named Joseph, who himself had also become a disciple of Jesus. This man went to Pilate and asked for the body of Jesus. Then Pilate ordered it to be given to him. And Joseph took the body and wrapped it in a clean linen cloth, and laid it in his own new tomb, which he had hewn out in the rock; and he rolled a large stone against the entrance of the tomb and went away. And Mary Magdalene was there, and the other Mary, sitting opposite the grave" (Matthew 27:57-61). With nothing left to do, the women went home to prepare spices and perfumes for the body. Presumably, the women slept little as the weight of what they had witnessed settled in on their aching souls.

2. Read John 20:1-10. Write a brief summary of the events recorded in this passage.

John 20:10 says, "The disciples went away again to their own homes." But Mary Magdalene remained. Her Lord had been crucified and now it appeared His body had been removed, possibly stolen.

3a. Read John 20:11-15. Two angels were inside the tomb. What did they ask Mary Magdalene?

3b. What was her response? Jesus spoke to her but she did not recognize Him at first.

3c. What did Jesus ask her?

3d. When the Lord spoke to her who did she think He was?

3e. How did Mary respond to the Man she assumed was the gardener?

We can only imagine the compounded grief Mary Magdalene was experiencing. She had witnessed the crucifixion and now the body of her Lord was missing. But then Jesus called her name. "Jesus said to her, 'Mary!' She turned and said to Him in Hebrew, 'Rabboni!'(John 20:16). At the sound of the Lord speaking her name Mary knew she was in His presence. This indicates the deep devotional level of her love for Him. Mary Magdalene was typically identified as the one "from whom seven demons had gone out" (Luke 8:2) even after her conversion. Here the Lord simply calls her "Mary." Perhaps He had been the only One who dropped her moniker in favor of her new position in Christ Jesus.

4. Read John 20:17-18. Mary must have nearly tackled Jesus, wrapping Him in a bear hug that indicated she would never let go of Him. What did He say to her?

Jesus orchestrated the announcement of His resurrection to be made to Mary rather than Peter and John who had been at the tomb just a short time before. Strange really, considering her past and the fact she was a women, that she should be chosen for the supreme honor of being the first to witness the risen Lord. Jesus was teaching a grand truth—He would build His kingdom with men and women, boys and girls. Whosoever wanted to come to Jesus would be welcomed and every believer would have a significant part to play in Kingdom work.

Jesus instructed her to go and tell the disciples about His resurrection. Perhaps it is a most fitting commission to announce His resurrection and victory over Satan since Mary had firsthand knowledge of demonic possession and just how formidable the enemy really was. Jesus had freed Mary from her demons; now by His death, burial, and resurrection, Jesus had vanquished her former tormentor once and for all.

5. The ramifications of the death, burial, and resurrection of Christ are so profound our earth-bound minds can scarcely comprehend them. Look up 1 Corinthians 15:54-57. What did Christ accomplish on our behalf?

The only right response is gratitude! "Thanks be to God, who gives us the victory through our Lord Jesus Christ" (1 Corinthians 15:57).

Beloved, rejoice and give thanks for what the Lord Jesus Christ has done on our behalf! Our God redeems. Our God regenerates. Our God restores. The only reasonable response is gratitude and joy. "Therefore, since we receive a kingdom which cannot be shaken, let us show gratitude, by which we may offer to God an acceptable service with reverence and awe" (Hebrews 12:28). Hallelujah! What a Savior!

FIXER UPPER

Mary's name has been irreversibly linked to her demon possession prior to her conversion. In a similar fashion, Rahab's name is virtually always connected to her harlotry despite the fact she was grafted into the lineage of Christ through her marriage to Boaz. Both women were tagged with the worst moments of their lives despite the dramatic change of character following their conversion. Beloved, if you are in Christ, you are a new creation (see 2 Corinthians 5:17). You are no longer defined by your past. Psalm 103:12-13 says, "As far as the east is from the west, so far has He removed our transgressions from us. Just as a father has compassion on his children, so the Lord has compassion on those who fear Him." Your present is attended by His presence. And your future promises to be glorious. 1 Corinthians 2:9 says, "Things which eye has not seen and ear has not heard, and which have not entered the heart of man, all that God has prepared for those who love Him." We are daughters of the King recreated in righteousness and truth!

DAY FIVE

Joy is not something we muster up or manufacture; it springs from an endless Source, Jesus Christ. Joy is the fruit of the Spirit of God, alive and active in us. He manifests the joy of the Lord in us and through us regardless of the circumstances of life. "The joy of the Lord is [our] strength" (Nehemiah 8:10).

Outrageous joy is the birthright of every child of God. It is a byproduct of our salvation through the Lord Jesus Christ.

- John 15:11 says, "These things I have spoken to you so that My joy may be in you, and that your joy may be made full."

- John 16:24 says, "Until now you have asked for nothing in My name; ask and you will receive, so that your joy may be made full."

- In Jesus' high priestly prayer, He said to the Father, "But now I come to You; and these things I speak in the world so that they may have My joy made full in themselves" (John 17:13).

Our study today is based in the book of Philippians, written by the apostle Paul. The hallmark of Philippians is joy. The word "joy" or a form of it is used over 15 times in this short epistle. Understanding Paul's circumstances and his staunch determination to experience the joy of the Lord despite them will aid in our study.

Paul had been arrested and placed under house arrest for two years. During this time he evidently was "welcoming all who came to him, preaching the kingdom of God and teaching concerning the Lord Jesus Christ with all openness, unhindered" (Acts 28:30-31).

The Roman government had seized the apostle and imprisoned him for preaching the gospel of Jesus Christ. Their intent was to destroy the apostle's ministry and frighten any who might be tempted to preach Christ. Despite his confinement, the apostle Paul continued to have a ministry. He was in chains, but the gospel was not.

In a twist of divine irony, the praetorian guards, consisting of some 9000 men, become his mission field. In 12-hour shifts, Caesar's elite military warriors were chained to the apostle. In God's sovereignty, the guards had become Paul's captives. Philippians 1:12-13 says, "Now I want you to know, brethren, that my circumstances have turned out for the greater progress of the gospel, so that my imprisonment in the cause of Christ has become well known throughout the whole praetorian guard and to everyone else." Many fell under the spell of God's servant, captivated by Paul's unstoppable faith, unruffled peace, and his unquenchable joy despite his difficult circumstances.

Paul was a man whose mind, will, and emotions had been captured by the grace of God. Obviously, his references to joy give testimony to the state of the apostle as he penned this letter to the church of Philippi.

1a. Read Philippians 4:1-3. As the spiritual father of the Philippian fellowship, Paul recognized his responsibility to address a problem. Disharmony has erupted. Who was squabbling?

1b. What instruction does he give to the ladies engaged in bickering?

We don't know that much about these women. We do know they are believers and they had shared Paul's "struggle in the cause of the gospel" (Philippians 4:3). They were church members, not outsiders. We do not know the nature of the disagreement, but we can rest assured it was not about doctrine. Had there been a theological dispute, Paul would have corrected the error. Therefore, we can conclude that the nature of the controversy was concerning non-essentials of the faith. We don't have much information concerning these women or the nature of their conflict. What we do know about these women is this: in the Holy Scriptures their names are forever linked with bickering!

Paul admonishes the church leaders to intervene and mediate to help the women move past their differences. The business of the church is in making the name and the glory of Jesus known. Energy siphoned off engaging in or in refereeing spats and disagreements is counterproductive.

2a. Read Philippians 4:4-5. What instructions does Paul give us?

2b. Why should we seek harmony?

The joy Paul calls for is not dependent on circumstances, but springs forth from a deep contentment and a solid confidence in the sovereignty of God. This lifestyle testimony validates our genuine conversion and points to the supernatural work of God in our lives. "Now as they observed the confidence of Peter and John and understood that they were uneducated and untrained men, they were amazed, and began to recognize them as having been with Jesus" (Acts 4:13). May others recognize that we have been with Jesus!

3a. Worry, fear, and anxiety are joy-stealers. The secret for living a life marked with joy is found in Philippians 4:6-7. What is the cure for anxiety?

3b. What is the result of taking our anxious thoughts to the Lord?

Paul's words here echo Jesus' teaching in the Sermon on the Mount. "Seek first His kingdom and His righteousness, and all these things will be added to you. So do not worry about tomorrow; for tomorrow will care for itself. Each day has enough trouble of its own" (Matthew 6:33-34). Rejoice in the Lord. Pray. Be thankful. All of these spiritual disciplines will usher the peace of God into your hearts and minds.

4. Read Philippians 4:8-9. To maintain the joy of the Lord we must dwell on those things that will point us to Jesus. What are they?

Beloved, as we renew our minds in God's Word we must seek to put His profound truths into practice. Paul wrote, "The things you have learned and received and heard and seen in me, practice these things, and the God of peace will be with you" (Philippians 4:9). Pray. Practice. Peace. The peace of God will guard our hearts and minds. The God of peace will be with us. This is Paul's blueprint for joyous living!

Do you want to know outrageous joy in the journey? Saturate your soul with the Word of God. Surrender yourself to the Spirit of God. Walk blamelessly. Work faithfully. War tirelessly. Live for the glory of God! Experience hilarious, outrageous joy in the journey.

Week 10
SELF-DISCIPLINE

DAY ONE

All discipline for the moment seems not to be joyful, but sorrowful; yet to those who have been trained by it, afterwards it yields the peaceful fruit of righteousness.

Hebrews 12:11

Samuel Taylor Coleridge is considered to be one of the most brilliant minds of the nineteenth century. A close friend of William Wordsworth, Coleridge is best know for his poems, *The Rime of the Ancient Mariner* and *Kubla Khan*. However, for all of his accomplishments, Coleridge always seemed to fall short of his full potential. He overslept habitually. He missed deadlines. He was known to leave his mail unopened in case it carried bad news. For half his life, he battled a debilitating opium addiction. He never wrote many of his best thoughts down on paper, leaving his more diligent contemporaries to write the poems Coleridge only talked about. He dedicated years of his life to a massive work on philosophy; it was never finished.

William Barclay writes this sad commentary on Coleridge's life:

> Coleridge is the supreme tragedy of indiscipline. Never did so great a mind produce so little. He left Cambridge University to join the army; he left the army because he could not rub down a horse; he returned to Oxford and left without a degree. He began a paper called "The Watchman" which lived for ten numbers and then died. It has been said of him: "he lost himself in visions of work to be done, that always remained to be done. Coleridge had every poetic gift but one – the gift of sustained and concentrated effort." In his head and in his mind he had all kind of books, as he said, himself, "completed save for transcription. I am on the eve," he says, "of sending to the press two octavo volumes." But the books were never composed outside Coleridge's mind, because he could not face the discipline of sitting down to write them out. No one ever reached any eminence, and no one having reached it ever maintained it, without discipline.[97]

Tragically, the story of Coleridge is the account of too many. They are full of potential that is never realized. What was the missing factor in Coleridge's life?

Self Discipline.

The Cambridge Dictionary defines self-discipline as "the ability to make yourself do things when you should, even if you do not want to do them."[98] Self-discipline and self-control go hand in hand. Self-discipline is a habit that is produced in direct correlation to our obedience as the Holy Spirit works in our lives, producing the fruit of self-control. The Greek word for self-control, *egkrateia*, comes from the root word, *krat*, meaning "to grip" or "take hold of."[99] This word describes those individuals who pay the price to get a grip on their lives and take control of areas that will yield success or failure.

The word implies self-mastery over one's inner desires, thoughts, actions, and words. It is the self-control we saw in Galatians 5:23 that a believer must exercise over his life.

Take a few moments for self-reflection before you proceed with today's study.

1. What areas do you have a "grip on" in your life (areas that you exercise self-discipline)?

2. What are some areas you need to "take hold of" (areas where you need self-discipline)?

Self-discipline is at the heart of success. Apart from it, we don't accomplish much in life. Individuals who have the *ability* to focus as well as define their priorities and *stay* within them tend to be very successful. If you take the "st" from *stay* and combine it with *ability*, you have the word stability. Self-discipline is the consistent stabilizer that is evident in every academic achievement, musical prowess, or athletic triumph. Accomplishment in the area of business or science typically comes to people who are incredibly focused and committed to their priorities.

3. Read I Timothy 4:7. What purpose does Paul give for having discipline in our lives?

Being able to discipline our lives is essential to spiritual growth. Interestingly, Acts 24:25 tells us that when Paul met with Felix, Governor of Judea, self-control was one of the subjects (along with righteousness and judgment to come) that he taught him.

4. Read I Corinthians 9:24-27. How does Paul challenge the believers at Corinth in these verses?

Relentless, rigorous, and focused. Those are the words that come to mind when I read these verses. And Paul tells them he practices what he is preaching. He does not simply go through the motions. He is serious about his training. He doesn't just "beat the air"! He disciplines himself with a stringent protocol so that he will not miss out on his God-called purpose.

5a. Make a list of the areas in your life (spiritual, health, education, career, fitness, hobbies, etc.) where you engage in ongoing training.

5b. In which of these areas does your training push you to stretch beyond your existing abilities/ proficiencies?

For the most part, self-discipline is not a natural instinct; it requires training. I was blessed to grow up in a home where self-discipline was valued and modeled. The word "can't" was not allowed in our home. Honestly, it never crossed my mind that I might not be able to do something. I might not get it right the first time, but "perfect practice made perfect." Quitting was never an option. My parents established clear boundaries and set high expectations for me. I cannot begin to count the number of times I heard, "If a job is worth doing, it's worth doing well." And it was expected that I would have a smile on my face while I was doing it! How grateful I am for that early training I received in the spirit of Proverbs 22:6! It has made an enduring impact on the trajectory of our family for generations to come.

John Maxwell makes an observation that is crucial to our ongoing training:

> If you want to make a difference and live a life that matters, you need to embrace some words and reject others. We all have a running dialogue in our heads. What we say to ourselves either encourages us or discourages us. The words we need to embrace are positive words, words such as *we, can, will,* and *yes.* What do we need to eliminate? *Me, can't, won't,* and *no.*[100]

Do the words we speak to ourselves move us towards becoming who God wants us to be? Are they words that we want to hear our children and grandchildren using? Are we speaking positive "becoming" words to those who are in our sphere of influence?

6. Read Proverbs 18:21. What does this verse tell us about the power of words?

Review the "running dialogue" that has been going through your mind (and often exiting from your mouth) for the last 24 hours. Are there some negative words/phrases that you need to eliminate? What are some positive "becoming" words/phrases you can use instead?

Negative Words	Positive Replacement Words

Self-discipline plays an especially important role when we find ourselves faced with difficult or dreaded tasks. It is what pushes us to do those things we know we should do but struggle to achieve. We discipline ourselves to:

- Get up early when we would prefer to sleep in.

- Read instead of watch television.

- Stick to an exercise routine or choose a healthy diet.

- Budget, clean the house, or clean out the garage.

I think sometimes self-discipline gets a bad rap because we associate it more with self-denial than we do with desirable outcomes. We fail to credit self-discipline for the stability it brings into our lives and our homes. We see it more as a negative than a positive. In other words, we see self-discipline as more of a legalistic "no, you can't do that," than a releasing "yes, I can reach that goal!" The writer of Hebrews addresses this tendency: "All discipline for the moment seems not to be joyful, but sorrowful; yet to those who have been trained by it, afterwards it yields the peaceful fruit of righteousness" (Hebrews 12:11).

My husband often told our boys as they were growing up, "You have to pay before you can play." In their early years, that often meant that they had to accomplish a task before they could do something they wanted to do. As they grew older, it actually meant the same thing, but on a deeper, more significant level. It meant they had to work hard to achieve the goals they wanted. Self-discipline is not a lock on a door that keeps us from something; it unlocks the door that frees us to become all that God wants us to be.

A hundred years from now, our lives will serve as either a warning (as in the case of Coleridge) or example (as in the case of Paul). A warning of the consequences of indiscipline, neglect, excuses, lack of direction and ambition...or an example of discipline, focus, and self-control.

Is self-discipline a fundamental Home Builder you are intentionally pursuing?

> The one quality which sets one man apart from another—
> the key which lifts one to every aspiration
> while others are caught up in the mire of mediocrity—
> is not talent, formal education, nor intellectual brightness—
> it is self-discipline.
> With self-discipline all things are possible.
> Without it, even the simplest goal can seem like the impossible dream.
> —Theodore Roosevelt[101]

DAY TWO

Yesterday, we defined what self-discipline is. Let's begin today's study by clarifying what self-discipline is not. It is not willpower. It is not self-dependence. Neither is it moral reformation. Any attempt at self-effort, apart from dependence on Christ is merely a self-focused pursuit.

Early in his life, Solomon asked God for wisdom and God granted his request (1 Kings 3:5-14). However, lack of discipline in his personal life marred his reign and ability to lead.

1. Read 1 Kings 11:1-13 and Nehemiah 13:26. In what area did Solomon lack self-discipline?

The Life Application Bible notes,

> Solomon received 'a wise and understanding mind' from God, but it was up to Solomon to apply the wisdom in all areas of his life. Solomon was obviously wise in governing the nation, but he was foolish in running his household. Wisdom is both the ability to discern what is best and the strength of character to act upon that knowledge. While Solomon remained wise all his life, he did not always act upon his wisdom.[102]

2. Read Ecclesiastes 2:10a, words Solomon wrote near the end of his life. What personal reflection did Solomon make?

Solomon's appetite of the flesh, his desire for women, lured him into a repeated pattern of sin. Like his father, David, the spiral of sin had serious consequences. But unlike his father, Solomon did not repent of his sin.

3. Read 1 Kings 11:3-9. How was Solomon's sin of polygamy compounded?

Sin always takes us further than we want to go, keeps us longer than we want to stay, and costs us more than we want to pay. Solomon did not exercise self-discipline over his desire for women. That lack of discipline led him to break God's law (Deuteronomy 7:3) and marry multiple women and take foreign women as his wives. Then his wives enticed him to worship false gods. And, his sin impacted the entire nation of Israel.

4. Read 1 Kings 11:12? How did God discipline Solomon?

The instability of Solomon's divided heart led to the divided kingdom, which eventually led to the nation being taken into captivity. Herein is an important life principle. *If we do not discipline ourselves, God will discipline us.*

Self-discipline is a serious spiritual issue.

In 1 Peter 1:13, Peter addresses the mindset of self-discipline, "Therefore prepare your minds for action, keep sober in spirit, fix your hope completely on the grace to be brought to you at the revelation of Jesus Christ."

5. In the twenty-eight words Peter writes in 1 Peter 1:13, he gives three commands. What are they?

    •

    •

    •

Let's take a closer look at each one of the commands Peter gives. First, *prepare your minds for action*. The KJV translates this phrase, "gird up the loins of your mind." We see a similar reference in the instruction regarding spiritual armor in Ephesians 6:14, "gird up your loins with truth." When a Roman soldier went into battle, he would take the four corners of his tunic and tuck them into his sash. He would make sure that all the loose ends were secure because he was headed into the battle. In 1 Peter 1:13, we see the same imagery used to describe self-discipline. Gird up your mind. In order to exercise self-discipline, we have to pull in all the loose ends in our thoughts.

6. What are some ways that we can pull in all the loose ends in our minds?

Second, Peter instructs us to *keep sober in spirit*. Keeping "sober" tells us how we pull in all the loose ends of our thoughts. A disciplined mind avoids the intoxicating allure of the world. Self-indulgence, the opposite of self-discipline was Solomon's undoing and will be ours as well, if we are not 100% committed to living a life built upon the priorities defined in God's Word. This is why biblical literacy is crucial.

7. One of the best ways to discipline our minds is to memorize scripture. What are two or three verses that you have memorized (or plan to memorize) to help you discipline your mind and reign in your loose thoughts?

8. Read 1 Peter 5:8. What reason does Peter give for maintaining a sober spirit and staying on the alert?

The enemy stalks us, waiting for any opportunity to take us down. We must take this battle for our hearts, minds, and lives seriously. God has given us weapons (Ephesians 6:10-20) and He expects us to use them to crush the attacks of the enemy. Disciplined spiritual warfare begins in the mind. Capture and hold captive every thought (2 Corinthians 10:5). Examine them against the Word of God. Are your thoughts lined up with His Word? If not, cast them out in the name of Jesus!

The third command Peter gives in 1 Peter 1:13 is to "fix your hope completely on the grace to be brought to you at the revelation of Jesus Christ."

When Scripture calls us to be vigilant in our battle against sin, it often challenges us to focus on our hope, the coming of Christ. In his article, *Self-Control: The Battle Against "One More,"* Ed Welch gives three benefits of meditating on the coming of Christ (underline mine):

> <u>First, [it] provides a deadline</u>. The battle with sin is hard, but on some specific day it will be over. If no end to our battle with sin is in sight, we easily can fatigue and give up, but when we know that the dead-line is approaching, we become much more vigilant. Like virgins waiting for the bridegroom or a student who must complete an assignment by a certain date, deadlines allow us to forgo sleep in order to do what has been asked of us. They bring an urgency to the present, taking away the typical self-talk, "Just one more _____, and then I will stop."
>
> <u>A second benefit to meditating on future realities is that eternity exposes those things that are important</u>. For example, sometimes our less-than-attentive consciences will permit "one more," but when we consider our thoughts and actions in light of the return of Christ, the self-serving nature of our desires becomes more apparent. A lesser version of this occurs even when we consider the advent of some other person into our addictions. For example, someone easily might justify a trip to a crack house (lover's house, bar, website, and so on) because it is just a short visit, just dropping in to say "Hi." But such thinking is checked when that person considers what he or she would do if a spouse or children showed up. If the potential appearance of a person can reveal the ungodliness in our behavior, how much more the coming of Christ Himself in person?
>
> <u>A third benefit of meditating on the grace to come is that it reveals our true destiny.</u> This can be a very powerful inducement. Our destiny is that we will be perfect creatures who do not know all things but are sinless. Consider that…Don't we often excuse our [sin] by thinking, "This is just humanness—we can't help it"? True humanness, however, is that we are created to be like Jesus in every way that a creature can be like Jesus. This means that we are becoming people who are controlled solely by the Spirit of the living God and not by our private passions. True humanness is being able to say "No" to ungodly passions, even when it hurts. [103]

It is significant to note that each one of these three commands in 1 Peter 1:13 requires a disciplined action on our part.

So, what is the motivation that would push us to order our priorities to make us self-disciplined? As we finish our study today, let's answer that question.

9. Read 1 Peter 1:18, Acts 20:28, 1 Corinthians 6:19, and Galatians 3:13. What is the common thread in these verses?

A scriptural understanding of ownership is what will motivate us to be self-disciplined. The bottom line? We do not own ourselves. This concept flies in the face of every self-help guru and middle of the night infomercial. But the truth remains; we have been bought with a price, a high price. As we read in Galatians 3:13, Jesus ransomed us by becoming a curse for us. The price He paid was His shed blood. We have been purchased with precious blood. Acknowledgement of His redemptive purchase is the place where self-discipline begins.

> If we do not sacrifice the natural to the spiritual, the natural life will resist and defy the life of the Son of God in us and will produce continual turmoil. This is always the result of an undisciplined spiritual nature. We go wrong because we stubbornly refuse to discipline ourselves physically, morally, or mentally. We excuse ourselves by saying, "Well, I wasn't taught to be disciplined when I was a child." Then discipline yourself now! If you don't, you will ruin your entire personal life for God.[104]

> Oswald Chambers, *My Utmost for His Highest*

DAY THREE

Most of us have laughed our way through the *I Love Lucy* episode when Lucy and Ethel are hired to work on an assembly line in a candy factory. Their job seems simple. As the candy comes down a conveyor belt, they must wrap each piece of chocolate in paper and place it back on the belt.

Their supervisor is one of those drill sergeant types who has no tolerance for mistakes. She warns that if a single chocolate gets past them without being wrapped, they'll both be fired. Then the boss roars out: "Let 'er roll!"

Suddenly the conveyor belt begins moving. At first everything is going fine, but then the conveyor begins to pick up speed. The faster they work, the more they fall behind. Trying to keep up, Lucy and Ethel hide the evidence. (I can hear you laughing as you picture what comes next.) Unwrapped chocolates are crammed in their pockets, under their caps, into their mouths, down their blouses—anywhere they can think to put them.

When the boss returns to inspect their work, it looks like they are doing a good job so she says, "Fine. You're doing splendidly." Then she bellows out to the conveyor belt operator: "Speed it up!"

Like Lucy and Ethel, do you ever feel like life is coming at you faster than you can manage it or have time to get it done? Each week contains 168 hours. If we categorize those hours in our minds, appropriating 25% of our week to work, we should have plenty of time to do everything else, right? Not!

In 1967, a Time magazine article noted that expert testimony had been given to a Senate sub-committee on time management. They predicted that advances in technology would radically change how many hours a week people worked. They forecasted that the average American would be working 22 hours a week within 20 years. "The great challenge," the experts said, "would be figuring out what to do with all the excess time."[105] Fifty years after that study, after all the major advances in technology – how many of us are wondering what to do with all the excess time on our hands?

For the past two days, we have been looking at the Home Builder of self-discipline. Time management is one of the most significant areas in our lives where we must exercise discipline. Our time is our life. Whatever controls our time, controls our life.

1. Read Ephesians 5:15-17. What insight(s) did you get from Paul's instruction on time?

As believers, our viewpoint of time management begins with God. As we saw at the conclusion of yesterday's study, self-discipline requires us to have a right view of ownership. We are not our own. Our lives, and consequently our time, belong to Him.

As Peter tells us, God is unrestricted by time, "With the Lord one day is like a thousand years, and a thousand years like one day" (2 Peter 3:8). However, our humanity binds us to the number of days we have to make an impact on eternity.

A. W. Tozer writes these penetrating words on viewing time from an eternal perspective:

> Because God's nature is infinite, everything that flows out of it is infinite also. We poor human creatures are constantly being frustrated by limitations imposed upon us from without and within. The days of the years of our lives are few, and swifter than a weaver's shuttle. Life is a short and fevered rehearsal for a concert we cannot stay to give. Just when we appear to have attained some proficiency, we are forced to lay our instruments down. There is simply not time enough to think, to become, to perform what the constitution of our natures indicates we are capable of. How completely satisfying to turn from our limitations to a God who has none.

> Eternal years lie in His heart. For Him time does not pass, it remains; and those who are in Christ share with Him all the riches of limitless time and endless years. God never hurries. There are no deadlines against which He must work. Only to know this is to quiet our spirits and relax our nerves. For those out of Christ, time is a devouring beast; before the sons of the new creation time crouches and purrs and licks their hands. The foe of the old human race becomes the friend of the new, and the stars in their courses fight for the man God delights to honor. This we may learn from the divine infinitude.[106]

What differentiates a biblical view of time management from a secular perspective is the source of all we consider to be significant. Our Source of life, the One from whom every resource flows is the Eternal One. By definition, a *source* is the place something originates. A *resource* is something available for use. In other words, resources are things we use and the source is the place where we get these things. God is our

Source and time is a resource He gives us to use.

2a. Before we go further in our study today, take a moment and consider these questions about your personal time management.

- Are you often late for appointments and commitments?

- Do you regularly miscalculate the amount of time it will take you to complete a task?

- Do you procrastinate on things you do not like to do?

- Do you maintain a written and prioritized list of things you need to accomplish?

- Do you have a time management system in place that works for you?

- Do you pray about your day before you plan it or plan it and then pray about it?

- Do you view time as a resource from God or as a ticking clock that is a source of stress?

2b. You do not necessarily have to write down the answers to the questions (although you may), but make some notes on your personal reflections in response to your answers.

For forty years Moses watched the Israelites waste time as they aimlessly wandered through the wilderness. His prayer in Psalm 90 records many of the spiritual insights he developed on time.

3. Read Psalm 90 and record every mention of time and take notes on what you learn.

The key verse in Psalm 90 is verse 12: "So teach us to number our days, that we may present to You a heart of wisdom." Did you notice the connection between time management and wisdom? Moses is saying that a proper value of time denotes a wise heart.

Sixteenth century French theologian François Fénelon wrote these sobering thoughts on the value of time:

> Time is precious, but we do not know yet how precious it really is. We will only know when we are no longer able to take advantage of it. Our friends ask for our time as if it were nothing, and we give it as if it were nothing. Often, our time is our own responsibility; we do not know what to do with it, and we become overwhelmed as a result. The day will come when a quarter-hour will seem more valuable and desirable than all the fortunes in the universe.

> Liberal and generous in every way, God in the wise economy of his providence teaches us how we should be prudent about the proper use of time. He never gives us two moments at the same time. He never gives us a second moment without taking away the first. And he never grants us that second moment without holding the third one in his hand, leaving us completely uncertain as to whether we will have it. Time is given to us to prepare for eternity. Eternity will not be long enough for us to ever stop regretting it if on this earth we have wasted time.[107]

4. What are some things that waste time? Those things that hold no eternal value?

5. Read 2 Corinthians 4:18. How do Paul's words help us to rightly frame "time wasters"?

6. Read Luke 14:28, Proverbs 21:5, and Proverbs 6:6-8. What do these verses teach us about time management?

 These ten "fixer-upper" tips (although not all inclusive) will help you to create a rhythm of stewarding your God-given resource of time to make an eternal impact.

#1 Plan your week. Every Sunday, take time to make a list of the things you need to accomplish for the week.

#2 Plan each day (making sure that your time with God is the first item). A daily plan is a microcosm of a weekly plan. Divide up the weekly tasks and assign them to a specific day.

#3 Schedule the essentials. Essentials are rooted in your priorities. - God, family, church, job, etc. Allow only things that matter to take up real estate on your schedule.

#4 Eliminate the non-essentials. Some things are important to do, but they may not need to be done now. You may want to consider keeping a waiting list of non-essential items and incorporate one or two of these tasks per week. (i.e. The coat closet needs to be cleaned out. But, does it have to be done this week?)

#5 Remember, your calendar works for you. Too often we fall into the trap of being pawns to our calendars.

#6 Avoid the hamster email/text message email wheel. Text messages and emails create the sense that our "on button" is always engaged. We must create margin in our lives. (More coming up about that in Week 11.) Build hours in your day and days in your week when you are disconnected.

#7 Learn to say "no". And make it your habit to pray before you say "yes".

#8 Avoid time wasters. Review the list of things you put on the list in today's study and be diligent to avoid them.

#9 Wherever you are, be all there. If you are home with family, be at home and engaged. If you are on a date with your husband or out with friends, be all there. If you are at work, be all in at work! Work hard not to be present in the body, but absent in the mind!

#10 Maintain a positive and joyful attitude about time and time management. Make sure you view time from a biblical point of view as a resource entrusted to you by God.

llllllllllllllllllllllllllllllllllllllllllllllllllllllllllllllllllllllllllllllllllllllllllllllllllllllllllllllllllllllllllllllllllllllllllllllllllllllllllllllllllllllllllllll

Lord, make me to know my end
And what is the extent of my days;
Let me know how transient I am.
Behold, You have made my days as handbreadths,
And my lifetime as nothing in Your sight;
Surely every man at his best is a mere breath. Selah.
Psalm 39:4-5

Week 10
SELF-DISCIPLINE

DAY FOUR

On May 30, 2010, a massive sinkhole, 60 feet wide and 30 stories deep opened up in Guatemala City, Guatemala, killing at least one man and swallowing an entire three-story building. Geologists believe that the sinkhole originated from a burst sewer pipe or storm drain that hollowed out the underground cavity and allowed the hole to form. Guatemala City is located in a region where the first few hundred meters of ground are mostly made up of a material called pumice fill that was deposited during past volcanic eruptions. The loose pumice is easily eroded, especially by running water. In the case of the 2010 sinkhole, the flawed geology was further compromised by the lack of zoning regulations in the city. The leaking pipes could have gone unfixed long enough to create the right conditions for the sinkhole. The underground erosion was invisible, but it was there all along. Basically, this catastrophe occurred because the city was built on a soft, unstable foundation and running water was ignored which wore away at what little infrastructure there was underground.[108]

What lessons about self-discipline can we learn from this disaster?

- Something can appear fine on the outside, but underneath, an unstable foundation is a disaster in the making.

- A small issue, left unchecked, can lead to calamity of major proportion.

How do we prevent a cataclysmic disaster, 30-story sinkhole size, from occurring in our lives?

First, we build our lives on a stable foundation.

1. Read Matthew 7:24-27. What do the wise and foolish builders have in common, and what differentiates the two builders from each other?

192

2. Using Scripture, describe what a firm foundation, a stable spiritual infrastructure, looks like in the life of a believer.

Second, we recognize the importance of small things. Sinful habits and strongholds do not just appear out of nowhere—they are the cumulative result of small concessions that ultimately yield ungodly behavior. Likewise, it is equally true that godly actions are the collective product of small, repeated choices that honor God.

Remember our definition of self-discipline? "The ability to make yourself do things when you should, even if you do not want to do them." Self-discipline is the muscle we exercise that helps us to live godly lives. And how do we strengthen that muscle? One small action at a time.

3. Read Proverbs 4:18-19. How does Solomon describe the path of the righteous and the path of the wicked?

At the end of Chapter 4, Solomon warns, "Watch the path of your feet and all your ways will be established. Do not turn to the right nor to the left; turn your foot from evil" (Proverbs 4:26-27). Our path in life is determined by the cumulative result of the daily choices we make. Repeated actions on our part become habits. Our habits determine the person we become.

Who do you want to be a decade from now? You are becoming that person (or not) through the choices you make today. You may wish to be a person who spends quality time with the Lord every day, exercises and maintains a healthy diet, and achieves personal and professional goals. But, have you taken any steps in that direction today? Our desires become reality through self-control and the key to self-control is discipline.

4. Who do you want to become? Create a profile of the person you would like to be in every area of your life (spiritually, personally, vocationally, financially, physically, relationally, etc.).

5. How does the profile you just completed differ with who you are today?

The distance between Point A (the person you are today) and Point B (the person you want to become) is bridged by self-discipline. And self-discipline begins in the little issues of life. In other words, there is value in sweating the small stuff. What are some examples of small things that make a big difference?

Set your clock and get up when the buzzer goes off so that you can begin your day seeking God.

Make up your bed. A discipline as small as making your bed can set the tone for order in your life the rest of the day (and will keep you from crawling back into it).

De-clutter your environment at home and at work. You will function better without the distraction of a messy surrounding. (Just a thought...If a pile has remained untouched on your desk for six months or longer, it can probably just be thrown away.)

Finish what you start. Some people's lives are just a long litany of things left unfinished.

Do the hardest task on your list first. That sense of accomplishment will bolster your energy to get more done. If you put off the hardest thing until the end of the day, you will find that you are probably too spent to tackle it. As Mark Twain said, "If it's your job to eat a frog, it's best to do it first thing in the morning. And if it's your job to eat two frogs, it's best to eat the biggest one first."[109]

Keep your word. If you say you are going to do something, do it. See your commitments through.

6. Now it's your turn. What are some other small actions that make a big difference?

"We must all suffer from one of two pains: the pain of discipline or the pain of regret. The difference is discipline weighs ounces while regret weighs tons."[110]— Jim Rohn

7. What are some small things you can do today to become the person you described in your profile?

8. Let's conclude today's study by meditating on Romans 13:14, "But put on the Lord Jesus Christ, and make no provision for the flesh in regard to its lusts." What is Paul saying in this verse?

- Put on Jesus Christ when you get up in the morning.

- Make Him your life.

- Be disciplined and make no provision for the flesh that would hold you to a lower standard or allow you to drift into sinful behavior.

9. How would "putting on the Lord Jesus Christ" daily build more discipline into your life?

As we clothe ourselves in Christ, He gives us the strength to do what we need to do to become who He wants us to become (Philippians 4:8). I love J. B. Philips' translation of Romans 13:14: "Let us be Christ's men [and women] from head to foot, and give no chances to the flesh to have its fling." Now, that is the way to live!

Father, thank you that I can clothe myself with Christ from my head to my foot and say no to the desires of my flesh. Be Thou my firm Foundation. Help me to stay on the path of righteousness and be disciplined in the small things so that my life produces big things for the glory of Your kingdom. For Yours is the kingdom and the power and the glory forever.
Amen.

Week 10
SELF-DISCIPLINE

DAY FIVE

Perhaps you remember his name from a high school or college literature course. More than likely, the sermon "Sinners in the Hands of an Angry God" would have been included in the study of the American colonial period. His signature sermon that sparked the First Great Awakening is considered the most famous sermon ever preached in America. And for many people, that is the sum total of what they know about Jonathan Edwards.

Born in 1703, Edwards was an intellectual prodigy who enrolled in Yale University when he was thirteen. He gave his life to Christ while at the university and answered the call to the ministry. A pastor and evangelist, Edwards authored dozens of books and later in his life, he became the president of Princeton University where he is buried. But perhaps his greatest legacy is found in his line of descendants.

Edwards' genealogy includes a U.S. vice president, three senators, three governors, three mayors, 14 college presidents, 30 judges, 65 university professors, 80 public office-holders, 100 lawyers, 62 physicians, 75 Army or Navy officers and 100 clergymen, missionaries and theological professors. [111] Mark Batterson writes, "Few Americans have stamped the collective consciousness of our country like Jonathan Edwards." [112]

Edwards' legacy did not just occur by happenstance. His life and the byproducts of it can be traced to a moment when Edwards, at the age of twenty, determined to live an intentional life to the glory of God. Edwards recorded his commitment in his diary:

> On January 12, 1723, I made a solemn dedication of myself to God, and wrote it down; giving up myself, and all that I had to God; to be for the future, in no respect, my own; to act as one that had no right to himself, in any respect. And solemnly vowed, to take God for my whole portion and felicity; looking on nothing else, as any part of my happiness, nor acting as if it were; and [to take] his law for the constant rule of my obedience: engaging to fight, with all my might, against the world, the flesh, and the devil, to the end of my life. [113]

As Edwards discovered, the hard work of leaving a legacy is found in what we do every day. This is the principle of *Leaving a Daily Legacy*, a daily stewardship that will write a story worth telling. While many people think about how they want to be known at the end of their lives, we must begin by considering how we show up every day. These are the moments that create a daily legacy.

If you would not be forgotten, as soon as you are dead and rotten, either write things worth the reading, or do things worth the writing.[114] —Benjamin Franklin

1. The following verses give us specific instructions regarding how we should view each new day. Make notes on your thoughts as you read each verse.

Psalm 118:24

Lamentations 3:22-23

Isaiah 43:18-19

Philippians 3:13-14

John Wooden coached the UCLA basketball team from 1948-1975. In a career that has been unparalleled in college basketball, Wooden won 620 games, including 88 games in a row. He won 10 national championships during his last 12 years with UCLA, winning 7 in a row at one point. How was John Wooden able to bring such success to the teams that he led? In a word, self-discipline. Wooden had as his personal motto, "Make each day your masterpiece."[115] Everyday, Wooden achieved *personal* victories before he led his team to victory. It was the victory he had over himself that allowed him to also help others become victorious. Do you have an intentional daily plan to make each day your masterpiece?

2a. Read Jeremiah 29:11. I know you are familiar with the words of this verse, but take just a moment and reflect upon them. Embracing the resonant truth of Jeremiah 29:11 is foundational to leaving a daily legacy. Do you wake up every morning wondering when the next calamity is going to occur? Or are you living each day with the confident expectation that God's plan for you is a future and a hope?

2b. What are some ways that anticipation and hope manifest themselves in your daily life?

2c. What keeps you from walking more confidently in this truth?

In the early church, when Christians wanted to order their daily lives around growing in Christlikeness, they would develop a daily order of living they referred to as the "rule of life." The Latin word for rule is *regula*.[116] The "rule of life" was a regular rhythm of life that provided stability. It was the discipline of creating a daily masterpiece for God's glory.

As we saw in week 4, Colossians 3 is ripe with daily rules for our lives. The key to creating a daily legacy, the believers "rule of life," is found in verse 17, "Whatever you do in word or deed, do all in the name of the Lord Jesus, giving thanks through Him to God the Father." The word *all* is defined as "the whole amount." [117] In other words, we are to live the whole amount of our day in the name of Jesus. John Ortberg writes, "Doing something in Jesus' name means to do it in His character. It means doing it as Jesus Himself would do it if He were in your place."[118] What would our lives look like if we lived every day as if Jesus was living in our place?

3. Think though your normal daily activities beginning with the sound of the opportunity clock every morning. What would doing "all in the name of Jesus" look like?

The only American missionary to ever be featured on a postage stamp, Frank Charles Laubach, served as a missionary to the fierce Moros, an Islamic tribe in the Philippines in the early 20th century. Known for the development of the "Each One Teach One" literacy method that has been used to teach about 60 million people to read in their own language, Laubach devoted his life to what he referred to as a spiritual experiment to live each day, every hour, every minute in the name of Jesus. In the early 1930's, Laubach wrote in his diary,

> For do you not see that God is trying experiments with human lives? That is why there are so many of them. He has [six billion] experiments going around the world at this moment. And his question is "how far will this man and that woman allow me to carry this hour?… For I who pushed life up through the protozoan and the tiny grass, and the fish and the bird and the dog and the gorilla and the man. … I have not become satisfied yet. I am not only willing to make this hour marvelous. I am in travail to set you akindle with the Christ-thing which has no name. How fully can you surrender and not be afraid?[119]

So the question is posed, How far will you allow God to carry you this hour, this day?

In a sense, each one of us is either creating an intentional daily legacy or generating one by default. The life story of King Jehoram, son of godly Jehoshaphat, is recorded in 2 Chronicles 21. Talk about a reign of terror! To solidify his power, Jehoram killed his own brothers (v. 4). Then he led Judah into idol worship (v. 11).

4. Read 2 Chronicles 21:20. How was his legacy described?

What a sad record! "He departed with no one's regret" (v. 20). Jehoram thought that living life his way would ensure his legacy. And it did. But, none of us wants to be remembered like that!

||||||||||||||||||||||||||||||||||||||||||||||||||||||||||||||||||||||||||||||||||||||||||||||||||||||||||||||||||||||||||||||||||||||||||||||||||||||||||||||||||||||||||||||||||||||||||||||

Spend a few minutes praying and thinking through your spiritual strategy for living every day in the "name of Jesus," a plan that will produce the harvest of a daily legacy. On first attempt, you may not create a "masterpiece plan" but you can begin to formulate a plan for what a Masterpiece day, an "all in the name of Jesus" plan would look like in your life. Design your plan in a way that you can track your progress, keeping in mind that self-discipline will be required. Good intentions are nice; intentional Godward living is our goal.

||||||||||||||||||||||||||||||||||||||||||||||||||||||||||||||||||||||||||||||||||||||||||||||||||||||||||||||||||||||||||||||||||||||||||||||||||||||||||||||||||||||||||||||||||||||||||||||

The self discipline you garner today to create a daily legacy will generate a lifetime of faithfulness, a series of daily masterpieces that when linked together yield what Eugene Peterson refers to as a "long obedience in the same direction."[120] The phrase actually originated from the German philosopher and noted atheist, Friedrich Nietzsche who wrote, "The essential thing 'in heaven and earth' is … that there should be a long obedience in the same direction; there thereby results, and has always resulted in the long run, something which has made life worth living."[121]

Nietzsche blew it when he announced that God was dead; but he nailed it when he pronounced that *a long obedience in the same direction* makes *life worth living* and might I add, writes a story that will be remembered.

Week 11
REST

By the seventh day God had finished the work He had been doing; so on the seventh day He rested from all His work.

Genesis 2:2, NIV

God Almighty. The All Powerful One. The Creator of the Universe. The Rescuer and Redeemer for all mankind. He rested. God had the Sabbath in mind from the very beginning. May God Himself be our example for building rest and margin into our lives and into the lives of our homes. So, grab your Bible, a pen, and a comfy spot and let's dig in to see what God has to say about rest. "I will give you rest" (Exodus 33:14b).

DAY ONE

Do any of you identify with these words from Job? "I have no peace! I have no quiet! I have no rest! And trouble keeps coming" (Job 3:26, GWT). I'm sure many of us are nodding our heads in agreement with Job's sentiment. I find myself saying so often, "I am so tired." "I am so stressed." "We are so busy." Anyone else?

In Hebrew, the word *menuha* means "rest". A well-known twentieth-century Jewish scholar writes this about the Genesis 2 passage:

> Menuha, which we usually render with "rest" means here much more than withdrawal from labor and exertion, more than freedom from toil, strain or activity of any kind. Menuha is not a negative concept but something real and intrinsically positive. This must have been the view of the ancient rabbis if they believed that it took a special act of creation to bring it into being, that the universe would be incomplete without it. What was created on the seventh day? Tranquility, serenity, peace and repose.[122]

Picture the sunrise, the sunset, the detail of a flower, the rolling of the ocean waves. In these masterful creations, we see tranquility, serenity, peace and repose. God desires the same for our lives and for our homes.

If God is omnipotent (all-powerful), why would He need to rest? Genesis 2:2 does not tell us that He <u>needed</u> rest. It simply says that He <u>did</u> rest. He teaches us by example. This is another reflection of His character which confirms His foreknowledge and attention to the details of our lives. What a good, good Father.

The word "Sabbath" did not appear in Scripture until the exodus from Egypt, but as previously mentioned, God introduced the concept of Sabbath rest from the beginning. The word for Sabbath in Hebrew is *shabbat*, which means *to cease, to stop, to pause, to come to an end*. Priscilla Shirer says, "He [God] wasn't tired. He was expressing satisfaction. Creation was complete, so He rested. And in doing so, He introduced the concept of rest to humanity. Rest was the capstone of creation."[123]

In the beginning, God sanctified and blessed the seventh day and set it apart from the other six days. It belongs to Him, not us. Pastor Steven J. Cole says, "On that day, we who are made in His likeness are to cease from the work of the other days and be refreshed in body and soul as we spend time worshiping our Creator."[124] If the Creator and Sustainer of all things took time to rest, then certainly I should do the same.

1. Exodus 20:8 says, "Remember the Sabbath day, to keep it holy." What does this look like in your home?

Holiness is a characteristic of God and something He calls us to as well (1 Peter 1:16). We put into practice and live out holiness when we obey God's command to remember the Sabbath. This looks different across denominations and even in Christian homes. It is important to seek the Lord's direction in how He would have you to walk in obedience to this fourth commandment from Exodus 20:1-17. Charles Spurgeon sums it up well, "It is good for us that we make the Sabbath a day of rest – a day of holy worship, a day of drawing near to God."[125]

2. Read Isaiah 58:13-14. What does this speak to your heart?

3. What presently poses a danger to your life when it comes to resting? (These aren't necessarily bad things.) What things can stand in the way of *shabbat*?

4. Why do we, as women, often shrink back from the idea of rest and margin? (Consider comparison, guilt, anxiety, etc.)

5. What does God's Word teach us about rest?

Matthew 11:28-30

Mark 6:31

Exodus 33:14

Hebrews 4:9-11

Galatians 5:1 tells us that "for freedom Christ has set us free" (ESV). He does not intend that we be enslaved by rules or regulations in regard to the Sabbath. This concept is not about following rules, but rather following Jesus Christ. We should observe the Sabbath and celebrate it with a joyful heart. God desires our worship. As we follow obediently in this area, we offer worship to our King and we are richly blessed with His rest for our body and soul.

Thank Him today for His promise from Exodus 33:14, "I will give you rest."

DAY TWO

What is your schedule for today? Write it in the space provided.

If you're like me, you probably need more space than the page provides. Do you have any room in your life? In your home? In your schedule? Is it so full and cluttered that you can barely breathe? Imagine laying in a hammock in your backyard, taking a bike ride, enjoying a quiet moment in the spring sunshine. Nothing to do. Nowhere to be. If you took a few minutes each week to do one of these things or something like it, would the world stop spinning? Ouch...my toes!

We all have plenty to do. We all have to-do lists. We all have commitments, responsibilities and obligations. Unless you're hiding in a dark hole somewhere (ooh, that sounds nice too!), life is pulling at you in some fashion. Are we missing something by constantly moving?

1. Read Psalm 46:10. Correct what's wrong with the wording below.

    "Be busy and know that I am God."

Don't you find it interesting that God tells us to be still? He knows us so well. He knew us before we ever came into being. And He speaks right to our point of need. To know that He is God requires being still before Him. Yes, we can pray, recite scripture, and sing praises as we drive, walk or run, but to <u>know</u> Him intimately requires a pulling away from all that pulls at us. If it didn't, He would not have instructed us to do so.

John Ortberg says, "The great danger is not that we will renounce our faith, but settle for a mediocre version of it. Hurry can destroy our souls. Hurry can keep us from living well."[126]

So how can we remove hurry from our lives? Let us look at our greatest example…Jesus Christ Himself. Ortberg goes on to say, "Jesus often had much to do, but He never did it in a way that severed the life-giving connection between Him and His Father. He observed a regular practice of withdrawing from activity for the sake of solitude and prayer. Jesus was often busy, but never hurried."[127] We would be remiss to overlook His example in this area.

2. What can we learn about solitude from these two verses?

    Matthew 6:6

    Mark 1:35

In keeping with our home building theme, I was intrigued by a note in *The Spurgeon Study Bible* on Mark 1:35. Think of this in terms of your children, grandchildren or those over whom you have influence. The note reads, "Very early in the morning, while it was still dark, Jesus was up at the sacred work of prayer. The more work we have to do with people for God, the longer we ought to be at work with God for them. If we plead with people, we cannot hope to prevail unless we first plead with God."[128] As I pray for people, as I lead my children in the truth of God's Word, as I hope to teach and influence others for the sake of Christ, I must first plead with the Lord. This beckons me to a regular practice of solitude as I approach the throne room of heaven in prayer and petition.

Does your hurried life cause you to feel disconnected from God? Do you lose your sense of closeness to Him when you're running to and fro day after day? Consider His example of solitude that we've studied today. Start by examining the time you spend with Him. Are you setting aside time each day to meet with Him…just you and Him? Are you going into that closet (that chair or corner of the couch) and seeking to know Him more? This discipline has truly been my greatest source of rest. He promises to give us rest if we will come to Him (Matthew 11:28).

For so many years, I did not discipline myself to spend time in His Word and in prayer. About 12 years ago, I made a decision to be a wholehearted follower of Jesus. As a new mom, I began attending MOMS Bible study at Bellevue Baptist Church. Through this ministry, Jean Stockdale encouraged and challenged me to get serious about my Father's business. I was raising and training boys for Kingdom work. How would I do this well without properly training myself? This process began by getting away from all the distractions of the world and being alone with my Savior.

Spending time alone with Jesus does not clear my calendar or shorten my list, but as I choose to be still, He reminds me that He IS God. He speaks truth to my heart and refreshes my soul. He gives rest to me when I am weary. He lifts my head when discouragement comes my way. He reminds me that a harvest is coming at the proper time if I do not give up (Galatians 6:9)! We cannot and will not experience true soul rest apart from solitude. If the perfect Son of God needed it, how much more do we!

3. Do you regularly make time for solitude? How often? Where?

Be on guard! We have a real enemy who seeks to keep us running the rat race. He knows if we continue our fast paced, hurried lifestyle, we will surely miss something God has for us. In his book, *Secrets of the Secret Place*, Bob Sorge writes, "Our enemy will do anything to get us to curtail the amount of time we devote to the secret place with God. He will push, distract, harass, incite, oppress, entice, weary, lie, intimidate – whatever it takes. Make no mistake, when you devote yourself to knowing God, all of hell seems to resurrect against you."[129]

4a. What are some common distractions that keep you from alone time with God?

4b. How can you guard against these distractions?

John Ortberg notes:

> Hurry prevents us from receiving love from the Father or giving it to His children. That's why Jesus never hurried. If we are to follow Jesus, we must ruthlessly eliminate hurry from our lives — because, by definition, we can't move faster than the one we are following.[130]

Truly my soul finds rest in God...
Psalm 62:1a, NIV

DAY THREE

Do you ever wonder why God gave us the Sabbath? Priscilla Shirer says, "God gave us the Sabbath to refocus our attention – to cause us to bring to the center stage of our minds and hearts the Person who we have placed at the periphery far too long. Margin keeps us from marginalizing God."[131]

As I read that quote, I admit a sting to my heart. I see how I sometimes allow life and all it entails to marginalize God and His intended role in my life. What does that mean? To marginalize means to "relegate to an unimportant or powerless position."[132]

Consider the account from Exodus 16 where the Israelites hoarded more manna than God had instructed because they were afraid of not having enough. They were more focused on the manna than on the Lord. They marginalized Him. They were distracted from His original intention, from His role as Provider.

1. What things can cause you to (albeit unintentionally) view God as unimportant or powerless? If He calls, does He get a "busy signal?"

Just as the Israelites fretted over having enough food to eat in the wilderness, our thoughts, anxieties and schedules can cause us to fret as well. While setting aside a day to physically rest is important, we can live a <u>life</u> of Sabbath that extends beyond one day a week.

Priscilla Shirer goes on to say, "When God is honored, when His authority is kept in proper perspective, all the blessing and favor He intends to give His children become a part of their experience. But when we seek to be our own sovereign ruler, we will find that we're working harder for fewer, less satisfying results."[133]

2. Pride can play a role in our busy lives as we seek to keep control of our schedules and commitments rather than submit to His boundaries. God honors humility. How can these principles from God's Word help us as we insert rest and margin into our daily lives?

2 Chronicles 12:7

Proverbs 11:2

James 4:6

1 Peter 5:6

The parable from Luke 8 about the farmer scattering the seed offers great application in the area of rest. It will be worth your time to read the entire text (Luke 8:4-15), but pay close attention to verse seven which says, "Other seed fell in the weeds; the weeds grew with it and strangled it" (Luke 8:7, MSG).

In reference to this text, Rick Warren says,

> Notice that this scenario is a little bit better than the shallow soil because the seed actually sprouts and grows. But the weeds choke it out so it never bears fruit. So many people hear God speak, but as they go on their way, life's worries, riches, and pleasures choke them, so they never mature. If you are always on the go and you can't hear God, you are facing the barrier of busyness. Often we confuse busyness with productivity and they aren't the same thing. If you keep going, going, going but you aren't spiritually growing, growing, growing, you are busy, not productive.[134]

Unlike a beautifully manicured and thriving garden, weeds do not require effort. They happen as a result of neglect. Distractions are much the same. We do not have to create or manufacture distractions. They are a part of life. If we neglect dealing with them, they will strangle us and choke the life out of us. Distraction harms our ability to listen carefully, to pray, to meditate and be still. This can be a spiritual danger if left unattended. And it can leave us feeling tired and weary, both in body and spirit.

Distractions can be a culprit in a life absent of rest and margin. Distractions can also reveal what we love.

3. Read Psalm 27:4. How does this verse speak to your heart?

Does the busyness of life distract you from God? Does the fast pace keep you from being still and knowing that He is God? Is pride standing in the way of submitting to God's timetable for your day? Are you tirelessly gathering and hoarding "manna" out of fear that God may not meet all your needs? Are you juggling so many balls that you have little time to gaze upon His beauty? Is your schedule and to-do list in the forefront of your mind most days?

The enemy wants nothing more than to keep you from drawing near to God. Remember, God's Word tells us to "come near to God and He will come near to you" (James 4:8, NIV). Drawing near to someone requires a cessation of activity. It requires a stillness, a pause. The same is true of our relationship with our Savior. If we succumb to a life devoid of rest and margin, we rob ourselves of the glorious blessing of nearness to Almighty God. The devil knows He can't snatch you from the Father's hand (John 10:29), but he also knows a hurried and hectic life will keep you from resting in the palm of it.

Third Day sings these stirring words in their song, *Your Words:* "Let me hear Your words above all other voices, above all the distractions in this world." [135] Take a moment to let those lyrics sink in.

Make a commitment today to intentionally remove some distractions and sit at His feet, listening to what He says.

DAY FOUR

Max Lucado quotes the following statistics in his book, *Anxious for Nothing*:

"The United States is now the most anxious nation in the world."[136]

"Stress-related ailments cost the nation $300 billion every year in medical bills and lost productivity, while our usage of sedative drugs keeps sky-rocketing; just between 1997 and 2004, Americans more than doubled their spending on anti-anxiety medications like Xanax and Valium, from $900 million to $2.1 billion."[137]

"People of each generation in the twentieth century were three times more likely to experience depression than people of the preceding generation."[138]

"The average <u>child</u> today exhibits the same level of anxiety as the average <u>psychiatric patient</u> in the 1950s."[139]

Lucado goes on to say,

Congratulations to us! The land of the Stars and Stripes has become the country of stress and strife. This is a costly achievement. How can this be? Our cars are safer than ever. We regulate food and water and electricity. Though gangs still prowl our streets, most Americans do not live under the danger of imminent attack. Yet if worry were an Olympic event, we'd win the gold medal![140]

Wow. I don't know about you, but those statistics are unsettling. How in the world did we get here? When we consider news feeds and tweets, smart phones and iPads, schedules and commitments, we begin to see how a lack of Sabbath living affects our lives. God instituted it and commanded it because He knew we needed it…for our good and for His glory.

At the time of this writing, life is in a bit of a whirlwind for me personally. I am anxious. I admit it. I will spare you all the details, but I have experienced levels of anxiety that are new to me. God's timing, as always, is so perfect. He has me digging into His Word and reading Christian books on this very topic at this very moment. After chuckling at His timing, I find myself overflowing with gratitude at His care for the details of my life. I'm studying and writing on rest and margin…just when I need to learn more about rest and margin. I'm certain another woman reading these pages shares my struggle. The aforementioned statistics certainly say so.

The Gospel of Luke cautions us, "Be careful, or your hearts will be weighed down with…the anxieties of life" (Luke 21:34, NIV).

1. What role does anxiety play in your life? What keeps you awake at night? What causes your chest to tighten?

Philippians 4:6 tells us to not be anxious about anything. In reference to this verse, Max Lucado says this,

> Be anxious for nothing. Nada. Zilch. Zero. Is this what he [Paul] meant? Not exactly. He wrote the phrase in the present active tense, which implies an ongoing state. It's the life of *perpetual anxiety* that Paul wanted to address. The *Lucado Revised Translation* reads, "Don't let anything in life leave you perpetually breathless and in angst." The presence of anxiety is unavoidable, but the prison of anxiety is optional. Anxiety is not a sin; it is an emotion. (So don't be anxious about feeling anxious.) Anxiety can, however, lead to sinful behavior.[141]

2. Read these verses slowly and in different translations. Make note of the promises in each. How do these truths speak to your heart as you consider anxiety?

Proverbs 3:5-6

John 14:27

Psalm 55:22

Anxiety often comes as a result of busyness and a fast paced, constantly moving lifestyle. It also plagues us as a result of unbelief or lack of faith in the sovereignty of God. To believe that God is sovereign is to believe that He is in control. Absolutely nothing in the universe happens outside of God's authority.

We act out of what we believe. Do you believe and yield to the sovereignty of God? What troubles you and causes you to be restless? Max Lucado offers this challenge, "Rejoice in the Lord's sovereignty. I dare you – I double-dog dare you – to expose your worries to an hour of worship. Your concerns will melt like ice on a July sidewalk. Anxiety passes as trust increases."[142]

Regardless of your age and stage of life, you are likely a busy woman. (If you're not, let's have lunch and I'll take notes!) Rest and margin are hard to come by. Hard to come by, but not impossible. God would not set an example and give a command that was impossible to follow. Be reminded of Jesus' words in Matthew 19:26, "With man this is impossible, but with God all things are possible" (NIV).

So how can we take Lucado's advice to expose our worries to worship? Consider praying back God's Word to Him. Repeat verses you've committed to memory. Recite those you've written on note cards. Thank Him for His character. Shuffle your playlist and belt out those Scriptures set to music and WORSHIP! Anxiety will melt away as He inhabits your praise and the enemy, who is determined to keep you preoccupied with something other than Jesus, will flee!

Rejoice in the Lord always. I will say it again: Rejoice! Let your gentleness be evident to all.
The Lord is near. Do not be anxious about anything, but in every situation, by prayer and petition, with thanksgiving, present your requests to God. And the peace of God, which transcends all understanding, will guard your hearts and your minds in Christ Jesus. Finally, brothers and sisters, whatever is true, whatever is noble, whatever is right, whatever is pure, whatever is lovely, whatever is admirable—if anything is excellent or praiseworthy—think about such things. Whatever you have learned or received or heard from me, or seen in me—put it into practice.
And the God of peace will be with you.
Philippians 4:4-9 (NIV)

The first step in a home renovation is a detailed assessment of what needs to be done. Spend some time today surveying the damage. Ask the Lord to reveal any anxieties that are contributing to the "run down" of your heart. Confess any unbelief, any doubt of His sovereignty. Lay those restless thoughts at the foot of the cross. Commit to a life of Sabbath rest.

Week 11
REST

DAY FIVE

God is the author of your limitations.[143] — Rick Warren

We know He is the Author of our faith (Hebrews 12:2), the Author of the Bible (2 Timothy 3:16), the Author of peace (1 Corinthians 14:33) and the Author of creation (Genesis 1:1, Colossians 1:16). But do we view Him as the Author of our limitations?

As we conclude this week's study, I want to share some practical ways we can build rest and margin into our lives. Pray as you read through these and ask the Holy Spirit to direct you, to be the Author of your limitations. (This will look different for each of us.)

- **Always make time for quiet time with the Lord.** Do not skip over this or push it to the bottom of your list. We <u>need</u> Him. In addition to still and quiet time in His Word and in prayer, find creative ways to infuse this into your already full day. Listen to podcasts in the car. Pray as you fold laundry. Sing praises while you clean. If intentional, you can rest in Him as you move throughout your busy day.

- **Take a bath or a nap.** Pull away from everything else. Take 15 minutes to rest and be still. It's okay to not fill up every available time slot in your day.

- **Unplug.** Have electronic free times and zones. (And I'm not just talking about for your kids.) Consider a block of time each day/evening where phones and tablets are put away. Stick to it!

- **Stay home.** We don't always have to plan an unforgettable event. Do you have a free Friday or Saturday night coming up? Leave it that way!

- **Say NO!** Have you heard it said, "Every need does not constitute a call?" You do not have to say "yes" to every opportunity. Saying "no" doesn't make you a bad Christian. Follow God's leading and specific callings for <u>your</u> life.

- **Prioritize.** Everything isn't urgent and most important. Think necessary. Think eternal. Next to your relationship with Jesus Christ, your family and your home should be at the top of your priority list. If these consistently suffer as you juggle schedules and fulfill commitments, you need to reevaluate the order of your priorities.

1. What are some of your favorite ways to rest and create margin in the life of your home?

Be prepared to share your ideas with your small group. The Lord may use your suggestion to speak to the heart of another woman.

In his book, *Anxious for Nothing*, Max Lucado shares the acronym, C.A.L.M., to encourage rest in our Lord and Savior Jesus Christ.

"**C**elebrate God's goodness."[144] The idea of shifting our focus from our stress and schedules to the goodness of God helps alleviate stress and worry and allows us to rest in Him.

2. Read Psalm 121:1-2. How was the Psalmist intentional? What did he know of his LORD? How does this speak to you?

"**A**sk God for help."[145] We do not have to (nor did God intend us to) do this life on our own. We cannot experience true Sabbath rest apart from a life entrenched in His.

3. What does the Bible teach us about asking for God's help in Psalm 50:15 and Matthew 7:7? Is there any uncertainty in these verses?

"Leave your concerns with God. Let Him take charge."[146]

4. Read 2 Timothy 1:12. How does this reinforce the truth that He is more than able?

"Meditate on good things."[147] Our thoughts matter. While we cannot control every circumstance, we can control how we think of them.

Celebrate. Ask. Leave. Meditate. CALM.

In this fast-paced, ever-changing world, rest and margin are going to be a continual struggle. It will never be easy to build these into the framework of our lives, but it is possible with the help of our God. If we seek Him, we will find Him (Jeremiah 29:13).

Priscilla Shirer closes her book, *Breathe*, with these words. I pray these words give your heart the boost it needs to pursue Sabbath rest for your own life and the life of your home.

> In every life there will come times that require us to fill our spaces and margins beyond those limits by which we have sought to abide. When this happens (and it will), don't get discouraged or off-track from your intention. Just refocus, reprioritize, and get back in step as you are able. And don't allow yourself to be overcome with a sense of guilt or condemnation. Remember: just as chronic overloading doesn't cause us to accumulate brownie points with God, short-lived overcrowding doesn't garner His disapproval. Your Sabbath heart will be seen and known by God even when your Sabbath margins are blurred and smudged by reality. God will know. He will know your desire to honor His sovereignty, and He will honor it with the nearness of His presence, the abundance of His grace, and the blessing of His favor upon all that you put your hands to do.[148]

This rest, we may conclude, must be a very wonderful one, since Jesus gives it. His hands give not by pennyworths and ounces; He gives golden gifts, in quantity immeasurable.[149]

–Charles H. Spurgeon

Week 12
HOSPITALITY

Let love be without hypocrisy. Abhor what is evil; cling to what is good. Be devoted to one another in brotherly love; give preference to one another in honor; not lagging behind in diligence, fervent in spirit, serving the Lord; rejoicing in hope, persevering in tribulation, devoted to prayer, contributing to the needs of the saints, practicing hospitality.

Romans 12:9-13

Hospitality is a God-commanded virtue. As Paul tells us, it is the essence of serving God. The word "practicing" in Romans 12:13 implies that hospitality is to be a continuous, ongoing action. Counter to the cultural trends of Pinterest and HGTV, hospitality is not an event. It is not something that happens just at Thanksgiving or Christmas. Hospitality is to be a habit, a distinguishing mark of Christians. However, it is a habit that is often ignored as Mortimer Arias notes:

> Hospitality is becoming an almost forgotten Christian virtue in our style of life today, particularly in big cities with their rampant crime on the streets, their locked-in apartments and all their affluent, urban and bourgeois devices which attempt to create privacy in our homes and our lives. In the New Testament, however, hospitality was a distinctive mark of Christians and Christian communities.[150]

John Piper defines hospitality as "the willingness to welcome people into your home (or your apartment) who don't ordinarily belong there."[151] This "willingness to welcome" occurs as we open our lives and homes to others in hospitality.

At its core, hospitality is walking in obedience to the command in Romans 15:7 to "welcome one another as Christ has welcomed you, for the glory of God" (ESV). It is rendering to others the comfort, encouragement, hope, and friendship that God has lavished upon us, and to the same extent. As we model the grace we have received from Christ and utilize our homes as weapons for the gospel, there is no limit to what can happen "for the glory of God."

DAY ONE

Simply stated, hospitality is the gift of love expressed best in our homes. Russell Cronkhite, who served three United States presidents as executive chef of Blair House, the guesthouse of the president, summarizes well the substance of hospitality:

Hospitality is a wonderful gift.
We don't need a grand palace, or a dream home—
few of us have those.
To make others feel truly welcome,
we only need an open heart and
the greater beauty of love expressed. [152]

Hospitality builds community and connection. Through it, bonds of friendship and fellowship are forged. As we open the doors of our homes to others, acceptance, comfort, and love are shared in one of the deepest ways possible. Max Lucado observes:

> Hospitality opens the door to uncommon community. It's no accident that hospitality and hospital come from the same Latin word, for they both lead to the same result: healing. When you open your door to someone, you are sending this message: "You matter to me and to God." You may think you are saying, "Come over for a visit." But what your guest hears is, "I'm worth the effort."[153]

To provide a backdrop for our study this week, take a few moments and think about a time when you felt welcomed into someone's home, a time when someone made you feel like you were "worth the effort."

1. Describe your experience in detail.

2. What did you feel and why?

3. Who contributed the most to your experience?

4. What do you remember the most about your time?

A home that says welcome opens hearts to real relationships. We want all who enter our little kingdom—family, friends, and guests—to know that they are welcome and cherished in this sacred place we call home.[154]

—Sally Clarkson, *The Life Giving Home*

Now, before we go any further in our study, we need to dispel a commonly held myth. Hospitality is not entertaining. Unfortunately in America, it has become common to use the word hospitality interchangeably with the word entertaining. As a result, we have placed too much value on entertaining and too little emphasis on hospitality. And there's a huge difference between the two.

- Entertaining seeks to impress; hospitality seeks to minister.

- Entertaining is about the host; hospitality is about the guest(s).

- Entertaining puts things first; hospitality puts people first.

- Entertaining points to us; hospitality points to God.

Karen Mains writes, "Entertaining subtly declares this is mine. . . . Look, please, and admire." Hospitality whispers, "What is mine is yours."[155]

When we view hospitality as entertaining, we put ourselves before others. And when we do that, we give legitimate footing to all kinds of excuses not to be hospitable:

"We're just too busy."
"My house is not nice enough, big enough, clean enough
 (or any other assorted "enoughs)."
"I can't afford to have people over."
"I'm not a good cook."
"It's hard at this stage of life."
"Having people over is exhausting."
"Hospitality is just not my thing."

The issue with all of our excuse giving is our attitude about hospitality. Hospitality is a close friend of humility. Where humility walks, hospitality will follow.

Rick Warren defined humility well: "Humility is not thinking less of yourself, but thinking of yourself less."[156] What keeps us from pursuing hospitality? Ourselves. We can become so full of ourselves that we simply don't have room for anyone else.

5. Turn to Philippians 2:3-7. As you read this passage, apply the truths Paul is teaching to hospitality. What would our hospitality look like if we emptied ourselves like Christ and made room for others through the ministry of hospitality?

Humility says, "I am willing to empty my heart of myself and welcome you in." When is the last time you were completely emptied of yourself as you engaged with someone? That is the humility and love that Christ showed to us as He emptied Himself, humbled Himself, and became "obedient to the point of death, even death on a cross" (Philippians 2:8).

6. Read Hebrews 13:1-2. What instruction regarding hospitality does the writer give?

Neglecting hospitality is the natural response of the flesh. When we put ourselves above others, we find that our tendency is to isolate ourselves from others rather than to engage with them. Note that the writer precedes his admonition on hospitality with "Let love of the brethren continue." Love and hospitality are interwoven. When we practice hospitality, we are putting human flesh on the gospel in a practical demonstration of love, the kind of love that God demonstrated to us. Dustin Willis and Brandon Clements write:

> The Bible begins with God making a home for humanity to dwell with Him in a garden and the Bible ends with God making a home for believers to dwell with Him in a city. These beautiful bookends to Scripture mean that not only did God do what He set out to do in the beginning, but somehow through all the mess of humanity, He actually made a home to share with us that is bigger and better than the first one…Throughout the saga of history, God consistently initiates relationship. He is a gracious host, constantly welcoming in wayward sinners who deserve His wrath—a people whose only hope is that He would show them undeserved hospitality.[157]

Peter echoes the connection between love and hospitality in 1 Peter 4:8-10 and then gives a very specific instruction for us to heed.

7. How are we to practice our hospitality? (v.9)

We can't just be hospitable; obedience is only part of the hospitality equation. Peter tells us we need to enjoy doing it. No grumbling allowed as we are mopping the floor. No murmuring accepted as we are cooking the meal. No complaining, period. As verse 10 explains, our hospitality is to be an extension of God's grace to us. Sally Clarkson writes, "When I see my home as a source of life to be extended to all who enter, I will put aside my own responsibilities in favor of doing the ministry of the home. I will be committed to the well-being of all those who enter."[158] She keeps a plaque on the piano in her home to remind her of her sacred task:

> To invite someone into your home
> Is to take charge of their happiness
> For as long as they are under your roof.[159]
> J. Brillat-Savarin

Do you view your home as a source of life? Do you find it easy to make room for others? When guests leave your home, do they feel like they were worthy of your effort? You don't need to record your answers to these questions. Just ponder them in your heart.

FIXER UPPER

When you encounter someone today (a stranger, a co-worker, a family member, a neighbor), engage with them. Make eye contact. Ask them some questions about themselves. Don't turn the conversation back to yourself (this may take a conscious effort). Just have an agenda-less conversation that focuses on the other person. Listen to what the other person says to you. After the conversation is over, walk away praying for that individual. If the person seems receptive, you might even ask, "How may I pray for you?" while you are engaging with them.

That's easy enough, isn't it? For this practice session, you don't even have to invite someone into your home (although you may). The object of this exercise is just to practice emptying ourselves so that we can make room for others. Make notes on your experience to share with your group.

224

DAY TWO

Hospitality in the Old Testament

In America, we have exchanged leisurely conversation on the porch over a glass of iced tea for texts with emojis and tweets limited to 280 characters. As a result, we have become a more isolated and individualistic people. American society today is pretty much the antithesis of the Ancient Near Eastern culture of the Old Testament. The Pentateuch (the first five books of the Old Testament) is full of rules and regulations regarding how to treat (not tweet) other people and the Jewish people took their responsibility for others seriously. As a result, hospitality was woven into the fabric of Jewish society. They viewed it as a sacred duty and cultivated a welcome in their hearts.

We find Old Testament examples of hospitality in Abraham (Genesis 18), Boaz and Ruth (Ruth), David and Mephibosheth (2 Samuel 9), and Elijah and the Widow of Zarephath (1 Kings 17), just to name a few.

Beyond examples, however, the Lord commands the people of Israel to be hospitable because they had been recipients of His gracious welcome.

1. Read Deuteronomy 26:5-19 and Leviticus 19:33-34. Make notes on the different hospitality commands God gives to the Israelites in these two passages.

In both passages God ties His command for hospitality to His act of redeeming His people from Egypt. John Piper observes:

> For the people of God in the Old Testament the duty of hospitality came right from the center of who God was. I am the Lord your God who made a home for you and brought you there with all my might and all my soul. Therefore, you shall love the stranger as yourself. You shall be holy as I am holy. Your values shall mirror my values.[160]

God reminded the Israelites that they had been foreigners who felt out of place in Egypt. He commanded them to show the hospitality they had needed and longed for during that difficult period of time.

2. Read Leviticus 23:22. What command did God give to them regarding hospitality to the poor? (For a beautiful example of this, read Ruth 2.)

As the Israelites obeyed God's commands, they became known as a hospitable people and in effect put His hospitality on display in the culture and time in which He placed them.

So the question must be asked, have you cultivated a welcoming heart? Can it be said of you that you put God's hospitality on display in the culture and time where you have been placed?

As we continue our time in God's Word today, let's look at three Old Testament examples of hospitality and the lessons about hospitality we can learn from them.

The first example of Old Testament hospitality we will look at is found in the life of Abraham. Abraham is on the receiving end of hospitality in Genesis 12:10-20 when he moves his family to Egypt to escape the famine in the land and from Abimelech when he travels to Gerar (Genesis 20). Ephron the Hittite also offers him kindness and hospitality when he allows Abraham to bury Sarah on his land (Genesis 23).

In Genesis 18, Abraham demonstrates gracious hospitality to three visitors who visit him by the oaks of Mamre. As soon as Abraham sees the men, his hospitality kicks in and he (with Sarah's help) hosts his guests with kindness.

3. Read Genesis 18:1-16. In what different ways did Abraham shower his unexpected guests with hospitality?

4. Now, read Genesis 18:1-2 again. What type of home was Abraham living in when this visit occurred?

That's right, he was living in a tent. Abraham lived a nomadic lifestyle and did not have a permanent place to call home. So when these visitors arrive, Abraham, ninety-nine years old and still recovering from his circumcision just a few days before, is sitting at the door of his tent. In the sultry heat of the afternoon, the air inside the tent would have been stifling. Sitting at the doorway would give Abraham some fresh air and perhaps the benefit of an occasional breeze. When his guests, heavenly beings in human bodies (more about that in a couple of days) arrive, he hosts them under the shade of the oak trees outside his tent.

Lesson #1—Hospitality is not about our homes.

Abraham's visitors were not looking to be invited into a perfect home. They needed a respite, a time of refreshing. And Abraham's hospitality offered them that!

In our modern day Western culture we think we need the perfect home before we can invite people into it. But, hospitality is not about inviting people into your perfect home, it's about welcoming them into your imperfect life. In our hurried and impersonal culture, people are looking for someone who will leave the to-do list undone in order to sit face to face and talk. The venue is irrelevant; the interaction between host and guest is what makes the lasting impression.

The International Standard Bible Encyclopedia describes Abraham's hosting of the visitors in Genesis 18 "an exquisite example of the etiquette of hospitality."[161] Exquisite hospitality under the trees outside of a tent? Yes, because the hospitality was not about his home; it was about Abraham making room in his life for his three guests.

Lesson #2—Hospitality is not about our food.

Don't get me wrong. Food is a great way to offer hospitality—relationships built feasting around the table are deep and lasting. But, the food is not the main thing, as we will see in the instance of hospitality offered to Elijah by the widow of Zarephath in 1 Kings 17.

At this time in the nation of Israel, things were not good. King Ahab and his wife Jezebel were tyrannical rulers. When they married, Jezebel brought with her a pagan religious system complete with 450 prophets of Baal and 400 prophets of Asherah. King Ahab stood by and watched his wife in repeated attempts to exterminate the worship of the one true God from Israel.

To say the least, God was highly displeased and sent his prophet Elijah to deliver a stern message to King Ahab: "As the Lord God of Israel lives, before whom I stand, there shall not be dew nor rain these years, except at my word" (1 Kings 17:1, ESV).

On the heels of delivering this message of judgment and anticipating a death warrant to be issued for the prophet, the word of the Lord instructed Elijah to flee to the safety of the Kerith Ravine where there was a water supply and where he would be miraculously fed. Eventually, however, even the brooks and tributaries of the Jordan River dried up.

The Lord then told Elijah to move on to Zarephath, a Zidonian town in the very homeland of his angry adversary, Jezebel. "I have commanded a widow there to provide for you" (I Kings 17:9).

5. Read 1 Kings 17:7-16. Describe the hospitality given to Elijah by the widow despite her poverty.

Imagine this non-Israelite widow as the prophet of Israel's God approaches and requests she provide him with water and bread, the customary comforts of hospitality. Hear the anguish in her voice, "As surely as the Lord your God lives" she replied, "I don't have any bread—only a handful of flour in a jar and a little olive oil in a jug" (verse 12, NIV). She planned to use these meager amounts to prepare the last meal she and her son would eat before they succumbed to starvation.

Realizing her plight, Elijah promised the impoverished widow that if she granted his request, she would not run out of flour or oil as long as the drought lasted. And in one of the most generous displays of hospitality in Scripture, she took him at his word, prepared him some food, and in turn, experienced the miraculous "hospitality" of God, just as Elijah had promised. The meal may have been meager, but the hospitality was abundant. Proof that hospitality is not about the food.

6. Take a few minutes to create a simple meal plan that you can use to host guests. Keep in mind, your hospitality is not about your food. Think about items you might be able to prepare ahead and don't forget about your crock-pot recipes. The less last minute food preparation you have to do will allow you to focus more on your guests as they arrive.

Our third example of hospitality in the Old Testament teaches us what is perhaps the most significant lesson.

Lesson #3—Hospitality is not about us.

Read the story of David, Nabal, and Abigail in 1 Samuel 25:2-38.

Nabal was a rich man. He had three thousand sheep, a thousand goats and many servants. David and his men were living in the wilderness where Nabal kept his sheep and they protected Nabal's herd and the shepherds who cared for them.

7. What request did David make of Nabal? (vv. 5-8)

In a time when hospitable treatment of others was considered a sacred duty, and those in need of food and shelter had a right to request it, Nabal (whose name means "fool") selfishly refused to share his plenty with David and his men.

Stung by Nabal's arrogance, David prepared to avenge himself (v.13). Informed of her husband's arrogant behavior, Abigail acted without hesitation and delivered a bountiful gift of food to David and his men (v.18). Most importantly, she approached David with an attitude of humility and self-sacrifice.

In the meantime, Nabal was at home throwing a party and getting drunk, so when Abigail returned home she waited until morning to tell her husband what had happened. When she told Nabal everything, "…his heart died within him so that he became as a stone"(v. 37). Ten days later, the Lord "struck Nabal and he died" (v. 38). When David heard that Nabal was dead, he sent his messengers to ask Abigail to be his wife. Because of her hospitality and humility, she became the wife of a soon-to-be king. Abigail understood the power of hospitality and her selfless response averted a crisis and elevated her to a place of honor. Unlike her husband, she knew that hospitality was not about her.

Hospitality is not about our homes.
Hospitality is not about our food.
Hospitality is not about us.

How can embracing these three lessons change our hospitality?

As we will see tomorrow, the Old Testament emphasis on hospitality will spill over into the New Testament and the early church. In the meantime, let's put God's hospitality on display!

DAY THREE

Hospitality in the New Testament

The New Testament is full of stories of hospitality given and received. The Middle Eastern terrain is rugged and difficult. Rocky hills and unforgiving deserts made travel difficult for the New Testament sojourner. Consequently, hospitality was an ongoing need. Cleansing for dusty feet, food, shelter, security, and conversation were some of the elements of hospitality a guest treasured.

However, the motivation for hospitality is what is most striking. Love. A welcome steeped in love was (and still is) the most valued gesture of hospitality.

1. Read Luke 10:27. Who are we commanded to love?

    •

    •

By practicing hospitality, we demonstrate our love for God as well as our love for others. As Alexander Strauch notes, "The Christian practice of hospitality was not viewed simply as a means of overcoming a practical problem. Theological statements by different authors in the New Testament show that it was frequently viewed as the concrete expression of Christian love."[162] When we show love to those around us, we are practicing biblical hospitality.

> …a person practicing Biblical hospitality should…be a loving person. This element separates Biblical hospitality from social entertaining or even distinguishes between the hospitality of a believer and an unbeliever. Believers can uniquely display God's love as they extend hospitality. Entertaining focuses on having a beautiful table decor or preparing gourmet food. Biblical hospitality is a demonstration of love. Food and other elements are merely tools used to express our love for people. Our motivation for being hospitable women is a response to God's work in our lives. Hospitality is one way we can tangibly demonstrate our love for God."[163]

2. What are some practical ways we can demonstrate love to others through hospitality?

3. Share a personal example of a recent time you showed love through hospitality.

When Jesus sent His disciples out to share the Gospel, the disciples being received in love, was a part of His mission plan.

4a. Read Matthew 10:11, Mark 6:10, Luke 9:4, and Luke 10:7-8. What instructions did Jesus give the disciples?

4b. What did He tell them they should do when people refused to welcome them?

Jesus Himself was often a guest in the Gospels. However, there was a wrong way and a right way to receive Him.

5. Read Luke 7:36-50. Describe the two different "welcomes" Jesus received in this passage.

Simon was a host who is not a "host" and the sinful woman was a "host" who is not even a guest. One of the underlying principles in the passage is, those who are forgiven most love most. What would our hospitality look like if we actually loved according to the degree to which we have been forgiven?

6. Let's look at some additional examples of hospitality in the New Testament and see what we can learn from them. Read the passages and complete the chart.

Some Examples of Hospitality in the New Testament

	Giver of Hospitality	Recipient(s)	Acts of Hospitality
Luke 19:1-10			
Acts 16:14-15			
Acts 16:22-33			
Romans 16:23			

In addition, Judas on Straight Street ministered hospitality to Paul after his Damascus Road conversion (Acts 9:11), Simon the Tanner welcomed Peter into his home (Acts 9:43), and the early church regularly practiced hospitality (Acts 2:42-46).

7. What are some other examples of hospitality in the New Testament?

"The first thing to remember on this journey [in hospitality] is the nature of God. He is sovereign, meaning He rules over all things. He orchestrates all things for His purposes, including who lives, works, and plays near you. You may not consider these people as gifts from God because they have been a part of your life so long that they've become a backdrop. You are prone to miss them. But every day you pass people who could be blessed through your hospitality."[164]

Make a list of some people who could be blessed through your hospitality.

Begin to formulate a hospitality plan for the people on your list. Make notes on your ideas.

Week 12
HOSPITALITY

DAY FOUR

Hospitality to Strangers

It is a worship service at Bellevue I remember well. Our former pastor, Dr. Adrian Rogers, was preaching and a fly kept buzzing around the pulpit area. I have to admit, I was somewhat distracted by the antics of the tiny winged creature. Suddenly, Dr. Rogers coughed and patted his chest. It was evident that he had just swallowed the fly. Never missing a beat, he quipped, "It was a stranger and I took him in." True story.

Honestly, I do not remember what the sermon topic was that night, but more than three decades have passed and I still remember how God spoke through the little stranger that was in our midst that evening. As believers, we are called to welcome strangers.

I grew up in a home where welcoming strangers was part of the norm. Sunday dinner and Thanksgiving, in particular, regularly included an unknown person(s) in our midst. Jason Foster comments, "Christian hospitality, as given to us in the Bible, is a sacred process of 'receiving' outsiders and changing them from strangers to guests." [165] My mother, in particular, has always been the master of helping that transformation occur. Time and again, people entered our home as "strangers," but they always left knowing that they had been honored guests.

The Greek word for hospitality is *philozenia* and is a combination of two words—*philos* which means "affection" and *zenos*, which means a "stranger" or "guest".[166] So the biblical definition of hospitality is showing love to strangers and guests.

As we have already seen, hospitality in the Old Testament was not predicated upon previous acquaintance. In fact, as we read in Leviticus 19:33-34, hospitality to strangers was a sacred duty. One theologian notes:

> It was and is felt to be a sacred duty to receive, feed, lodge, and protect any traveler who might stop at the door. The stranger was treated as a guest and men who had thus eaten together were bound to each other by the strongest ties of friendship, which descended to their heirs, confirmed by mutual presents.[167]

What actually happened is that people travelling by would just sit down at the door of a total stranger until the head of the household would come to the door and invite them in for the evening meal. In Job 31:32, Job referenced this custom explaining that he had always been careful to practice hospitality, "The alien has not lodged outside, for I have opened my doors to the traveler." We saw another example of hospitality to strangers in Genesis 18 when Abraham welcomed the three angel/visitors.

1. Turn back to Genesis 18:2. What did Abraham do when he saw the strangers approaching his tent?

Abraham is genuinely glad to see these visitors. In the form of bowing Abraham assumed, the person bowing "falls upon the knees, and then gradually inclines the body until the head touches the ground."[168] By taking this position, Abraham is letting them know that their presence as guests is a personal favor to him.

2. Explore these similar examples in the Old Testament when hospitality was offered to strangers. Make notes on who offered the hospitality and who was on the receiving end.

Genesis 19:1-3

Judges 6:11-24

Judges 13:2-20

The writer of Hebrews was referencing these host-stranger encounters when he noted that some have "entertained angels without knowing it" (13:2). He was encouraging the recipients of his letter to regularly practice hospitality, not because they would necessarily have a supernatural guest visit their home, but because he wanted them to know that hospitality practiced often resulted in an unexpected blessing.

3. Consider the hospitality given to strangers in the next two passages, making notes on the kindness extended to the individual(s).

Exodus 2:15-21

Joshua 2

Both Moses and the two spies were in desperate need of hospitality, in fact, their lives depended upon receiving kindness from someone they had never met before.

The Old Testament is full of examples of hospitality being given to strangers who become valued guests and the New Testament is no different. Among both Jews and Greeks, hospitality to strangers was considered to be a moral obligation. Over and over again in the New Testament we see hospitality extended by believers to others without distinction.

Jesus often reached people through hospitality. While the religious leaders of his day did not want to have their reputations tarnished by being seen with those they considered beneath them, Jesus regularly accepted invitations to eat with tax collectors and public sinners (Mark 2:16, Luke 19:1-10).

4. Read Luke 14:12-14. What did Jesus say about welcoming the unwelcome?

As Jesus teaches His disciples, biblical hospitality is different from the world's hospitality because it is offered to the downtrodden and often unwanted people who have little to offer in return. Alexander Strauch observes, "For many people, hospitality is practiced only to meet their own social needs. Sometimes it is a self-glorifying show to impress others with one's home or entertainment skills. In contrast, Christian hospitality is humble, sacrificial service."[169] And when we welcome the unwelcome, when we extend hospitality to strangers, we are actually offering hospitality to Jesus as He explains in Matthew 25:34-46.

5. Read Matthew 25:34-40. List the specific ways Jesus says we are to minister to the "least of them."

6. How can embracing the truth of our Savior's words in Matthew 25 be reflected in our hospitality to the needy?

Hospitality that included those who are outside the circle of close family and friends was the mandate of Paul's command in Romans 12:13 when he exhorted the church at Rome to contribute "to the needs of the saints, practicing hospitality."

To fully understand what Paul is saying, let's backtrack to the opening admonition in Romans 12:1-2.

> Therefore I urge you, brethren, by the mercies of God, to present your bodies a living and holy sacrifice, acceptable to God, which is your spiritual service of worship. And do not be conformed to this world, but be transformed by the renewing of your mind, so that you may prove what the will of God is, that which is good and acceptable and perfect.

After Paul's opening statement, he then lists practical ways to have a renewed mind and live in conformity to God's will. Practicing hospitality is one of the ways Paul says we demonstrate that we have a transformed mind. The word "practicing" in verse 13 can also be translated "pursue". As we become a "living and holy sacrifice" we will pursue ways to demonstrate hospitality to everyone, even strangers.

As Paul concludes his letter to the church at Rome, he circles back to the subject of hospitality with specific instructions regarding a visiting sister they do not know, Phoebe.

7. Read Romans 16:1-2. Practically, what would that hospitality to Phoebe look like?

When we reach out to others and lavish them with love, we are living out the Gospel. As we conclude our study today, let's reflect on this challenge from Henry Nouwen:

> Although many, we might even say most, strangers in this world become easily the victim of a fearful hostility, it is possible for men and women and obligatory for Christians to offer an open and hospitable space where strangers can cast off their strangeness and become our fellow human beings.[170]

Helping strangers "cast off their strangeness" might just be my favorite description of hospitality. As we have seen today, Scripture calls us to a place where we meet others in their difficulty, in their brokenness, in their pain. And as we do that, we point them to the One who can make them whole and meet them at their deepest need.

DAY FIVE

Intentional Hospitality

In his book, *Intentional Living: Choosing a Life That Matters*, John Maxwell makes it clear that there is a big difference between good intentions and being intentional. Maxwell writes:

> ...if all you ever do is cultivate good intentions, but you never act with intentionality, you're actually likely to become more frustrated and less fulfilled, because your desire for positive change may increase, but the lack of results will leave you frustrated. Whether we realize it or not, people live in one land or the other...we either settle for good intentions or embrace intentional living.[171]

Hospitality is an area, in which many of us have good intentions, but life happens and we simply don't follow through. And more and more, we find ourselves drifting toward shallow, superficial relationships that are driven by our fast-paced lives and overbooked schedules. We have crowded our lives with so many things that we take little time out to linger with family and friends.

At Bellevue, one of our values is Intentional Hospitality, welcoming every person with the love of Jesus. Intentional hospitality is not just something we should do at church; it should be the everyday "welcome" every guest encounters in our homes. One of the best examples of intentional hospitality in the Bible occurred in Bethany, a small village that was about a two-mile walk from Jerusalem.

1. Read Luke 10:38-42, the familiar story when Jesus was a guest in the home of Martha and Mary. Fill in the blanks below.

   Mary was _____ (v. 39). Martha was _____.

Luke's contrasting descriptions of the two women provide us with some meaningful insight into hospitality.

2. What was Martha focused on?

Before we go any further, let's be clear. There is nothing wrong with cleaning our homes or preparing a good meal for our guests. However, those activities are only a backdrop to the greater story that will unfold in our homes through intentional hospitality. If we are overly consumed, if we are distracted, by providing a perfect meal, we will miss the opportunity to share the Bread of Life with our guests.

Notice how quickly Martha transitions from being distracted to being upset. And then observe how easily her emotions manifest themselves through grumbling and complaining. As we saw in 1 Peter 4:9, that was not the way to practice hospitality. Sometimes hospitality is inconvenient and most of the time, it requires extra work. But, we are called to be hospitable regardless. Alexander Strauch addresses this:

> The opposite of complaining is gladness – the willingness to cheerfully accept the inconvenience, labor, and cost of hospitality. Hospitality is a form of giving, and "God loves a cheerful giver" (2 Corinthians 9:7, NASB). So let us ask God to give us a cheerful spirit as we practice hospitality.

> Certainly the ministry (and corresponding inconveniences) of hospitality can easily rattle our grumbling bones. Hospitality demands old-fashioned work. It may be costly and is often inconvenient. It is time-consuming. It places strain on the family. Sometimes guests abuse their Christian brothers' and sisters' hospitality. And during times of persecution, hospitality can even be dangerous.

> Hospitality, therefore, is a concrete, down-to-earth test of our fervent love for God and His people. Love can be an abstract, indistinct idea; hospitality is specific and tangible. We seldom complain about loving others too much, but we do complain about the inconveniences of hospitality. Hospitality is love in action. Hospitality is the flesh and muscle on the bones of love. Through caring acts of hospitality, the reality of our love is tested.[172]

Martha had good intentions, but she was not intentional in her hospitality. Now, let's switch our attention to Mary.

3. Who was Mary focused on?

Mary had a hungry heart. She did not want to miss a thing Jesus said and soaked up every moment in His presence. She was so captivated by Him that she totally missed all the fuss going on in the kitchen.

4. What admonition did Jesus give to Martha?

There was nothing wrong with *what* Martha was doing; the problem was *how* she was doing it. Jesus was correcting Martha about her attitude. She was serving the Lord, but her out of balance preoccupation with the details was robbing her of her joy in serving. She had allowed the minutiae of hospitality to replace righteousness, peace, joy and love and in doing so, missed "the one thing" she needed.

As Martha discovered, the right thing done the wrong way is always wrong. In Romans 14:17-20a, Paul provides further caution:

"For the kingdom of God is not a matter of eating and drinking, but of righteousness, peace and joy in the Holy Spirit, because anyone who serves Christ in this way is pleasing to God and receives human approval. Let us therefore make every effort to do what leads to peace and to mutual edification. Do not destroy the work of God for the sake of food" (NIV).

5. How would taking into account Jesus' words to Martha and Paul's instruction in Romans 14 change your thoughts and actions regarding hospitality?

Offering hospitality gives us opportunities to check our hearts to make sure we don't miss "the one thing" that is necessary. We need to ask ourselves questions such as:

- Are we complaining in our hearts about opening our homes to others?

- Have the details of our hospitality consumed us?

- Does our hospitality distract us from engaging with people?

- Do we care more about the way our home looks or how our food tastes than we do about exalting Christ?

Martha apparently learned from her experience because things are different when she and Mary open up their home to Jesus and His disciples when the last Passover they would share together was approaching. (Side Note: This dinner took place the week after Jesus had raised their brother, Lazarus from the dead. Imagine what it was like to be a guest at that table. You look over at Lazarus and ask, "Have you had a good week?" He answers, "Well, I got sick and died and after three days Jesus stopped by the cemetery and shouted out, 'Lazarus come forth!' and I did. How was your week?")

6a. Read John 12:1-11. What is Martha doing during supper?

6b. What does Mary do during the meal?

Martha is still serving and Mary is still at the feet of Jesus, but things have changed. Martha is not grumbling as she serves. She seems to have accepted that she was honoring Jesus through serving dinner while Mary was honoring Him by anointing Him with the costly perfume. Both women were being intentional in their hospitality. And their love showed.

‖‖

FIXER UPPER

The tips on the following pages are some practical strategies that will help both the Mary's and Martha's among us to be more intentional in our hospitality.

Top Ten Hospitality Items:

(While you don't have to have these things to practice hospitality, collecting these items will make your hospitality easier.)

1. Dishes – Have enough on hand to serve as many as your table(s) will hold. White dishes are timeless and can be used with any color scheme. I have a set of 20 white plates and bowls that I picked up at a garage sale. For seasonal colored dinnerware, my favorite spot to shop is Dollar Tree.

2. Silverware – Again, make sure you have enough to serve as many as your home will accommodate.

3. Glasses – Don't spend too much on these, in case they break. Dollar Tree, Wal-Mart, and IKEA have reasonable options.

4. Baskets – I grab nice baskets at garage sales and use them for bread, crackers, chips, buns, flower arrangements, etc.

5. Serving Ware – Look for serving platters and dishes at thrift stores and garage sales. White, clear, and pewter are my favorite serving pieces because they can be used for any occasion.

6. Pitchers – Having a water/tea pitcher close by allows for easy refills. For water, float lemons, limes, or blackberries for added color.

7. Tablecloths – Depending on your style, tablecloths are a nice addition to your hospitality collection. Placemats, burlap runners, and chargers are good options as well.

8. Decorative items – If you collect seasonal décor and display it throughout your home, you will be ready to extend hospitality at a moment's notice. I keep items in Rubbermaid tubs (labeled by the season) and just pull them out and decorate by season. Tip: Take pictures and refer to them so that you don't have to recreate every year.

9. Fresh flowers and candles – Both are inexpensive ways to create a welcoming atmosphere in your home.

10. Paper or cloth napkins – Buy these on sale and have them on hand to use so that you don't have to run out at the last minute looking for them.

Top Ten Hospitality Tips:

1. Create a welcoming scent. Light candles, bake cookies, brew a pot of coffee or warm apple cider in a pot on the stove.

2. Have snacks available when your guests arrive. Light appetizers give your guests something to do and a place to hang out while others are arriving and you are putting the finishing touches on the meal.

3. Be familiar with your guests' food preferences (including allergies) and take those into account when you plan your menu.

4. Play music. It creates a relaxing atmosphere.

5. Use inviting lighting. Lamps and candles provide a warm, inviting feel.

6. Have a plan for something to do after you eat. Board games and fire pits give great opportunities for conversation. Remember to be intentional to move conversation toward the gospel and/or spiritual things.

7. Put the pre-meal dishes in the dishwasher and run them during the meal. This will make the after-meal cleanup easier.

8. Look at your front door. Does it communicate welcome to your guests? A nice doormat, a plant, a pumpkin in the fall, a Christmas wreath all help warm up the entrance to your home.

9. Pay attention to the bathroom your guests will use. A nice guest towel, a candle, and hand soap are inexpensive, but welcoming additions.

10. Keep the meal simple. Your guests came because they wanted to spend time with you.

What are some additional tips you can share with your small group?

Additional Resources on Hospitality:

Open Heart, Open Home, Karen Mains

Practicing Hospitality: The Joy of Serving Others, Pat Enis and Lisa Tatlock

The Home Experience, Devi Titus and Marilyn Weiner

The Hospitality Commands, Alexander Strauch

The Life Giving Home, Sally and Sarah Clarkson

The Life Giving Table, Sally Clarkson

The Simplest Way to Change the World, Dustin Willis and Brandon Clements

HOW TO BECOME A CHRISTIAN

Dear one, has there ever been a time that you have given your heart to the Lord? Do you have the assurance that if you were to die right now, you would go straight to heaven to spend all eternity in the presence of the Lord Jesus Christ and all His followers? If not, please let me share with you how you can be saved.

Admit Your Sin

First, you must understand that you are a sinner. The Bible says, *All have sinned and fall short of the glory of God* (Rom. 3:23). In Romans 6:23 the Bible says, *For the wages of sin is death.* That means that sin has separated us from a Holy God and we are under the sentence of eternal death and separation from God.

Abandon Self-Effort

Secondly, you must understand that you cannot save yourself by your own efforts. The Bible is very clear that it is *not by works of righteousness which we have done, but according to His mercy He saved us* (Titus 3:5). Again, in Ephesians 2:8-9 the Bible says, *For by grace you have been saved through faith; and that not of yourselves, it is the gift of God; not as a result of works, that no one should boast.*

Acknowledge Christ's Payment

Thirdly, you must believe that Jesus Christ, the Son of God, died for your sins. The Bible says, *God demonstrates His own love toward us, in that while we were yet sinners, Christ died for us* (Rom. 5:8). That means He died a sacrificial death in your place. Your sin debt has been paid by the blood of Jesus Christ, which *cleanses us from all sin* (I John 1:7).

Accept Him as Savior

Fourthly, you must put your faith in Jesus Christ and Him alone for your salvation. The blood of Christ does you no good until you receive Him by faith. The Bible says, *Believe on the Lord Jesus Christ, and you shall be saved* (Acts 16:31).

Has there been a time in your life that you have taken this all-important step of faith? If not, I urge you to do it right now. Jesus Christ is the only way to heaven. He said, *"I am the way, the truth, and the life; no man comes unto the Father, but by Me"* (John 14:16).

Would you like to become a Christian? Would you like to invite Jesus Christ to come into your heart today? Read over this prayer and if it expresses the desire of your heart, you may ask Him into your heart to take away your sin, fill you with His Spirit, and take you to home to heaven when you die. If this is your intention, pray this prayer.

"Oh God, I'm a sinner. I am lost and I need to be saved. I know I cannot save myself, so right now, once and for all, I trust You to save me. Come into my heart, forgive my sin, and make me Your child. I give you my life. I will live for You as You give me Your strength. Amen"

If you will make this your heartfelt prayer, God will hear and save you! Jesus has promised that He will never leave nor forsake anyone who comes to Him in faith. In John 6:37 He said, *"The One who comes to Me I will certainly not cast out."*

Welcome to the family!

END NOTES

Introduction

1. Clarkson, S. & Clarkson, S. (2015). *The Life Giving Home,* p. 14. Carol Stream, IL: Tyndale House Publishing.

2. Clarkson, S. & Clarkson, S. (2015). *The Life Giving Home,* p. 14. Carol Stream, IL: Tyndale House Publishing.

3. Smith, C.C. & Pattison, J. (2014). *Slow Church: Cultivating Community in the Patient Way of Jesus,* p. 62. Downer's Grove, IL: InterVarsity Press.

4. Schlabach, G. (1998). The Vow of Stability. *Gerald Schlabach.* Retrieved from http://www.geraldschlabach.net/the-vow-of-stability/

5. Stability. (n.d.). *Merriam-Webster Dictionary.* Retrieved from https://www.merriam-webster.com/dictionary/stability

6. Schaeffer, E. (1975). *What is a Family?,* p. 122. Grand Rapids, MI: Baker Books.

7. Lewis, C.S. (1996). *Mere Christianity,* p. 176. New York, NY: Touchstone.

Week 2

8. Wisdom. (n.d.). *Merriam-Webster Dictionary.* Retrieved from https://www.merriam-webster.com/dictionary/wisdom

9. Chambers, O. (2015). *The Highest Good-The Pilgrim's Songbook*, p. 537. Grand Rapids, MI:Discovery House.

10. Tozer, A. W. (1961). *The Knowledge of the Holy*, p. 110-111. New York, NY: Harper Collins Publishers.

11. Gaines, D. (2017) *Choose Wisely, Live Fully*, p. 44. Nashville, TN: Abingdon Press.

12. *The ESV Study Bible*, p. 144. Wheaton, IL: Crossway.

13. Drummond, L., Drummond, B. (1997). *Women of Awakenings*, p. 36. Grand Rapids, MI: Kregel Publications.

14. Drummond, L., Drummond, B. (1997). *Women of Awakenings*, p. 40. Grand Rapids, MI: Kregel Publications.

15. Ortberg, J. (1997). *The Life You're Always Wanted*, p. 81. Grand Rapids, MI: Zondervan.

16. Metaxas, E. (2015). *7 Women*, p. 59. Nashville, TN: Nelson Books.

17. Metaxas, E. (2015). *7 Women*, p. 76-78. Nashville, TN: Nelson Books.

18. Metaxas, E. (2015). *7 Women*, p. 139. Nashville, TN: Nelson Books.

19. Metaxas, E. (2015). *7 Women*, p. 139. Nashville, TN: Nelson Books.

20. Metaxas, E. (2015). *7 Women*, p. 143. Nashville, TN: Nelson Books.

21. Metaxas, E. (2015). *7 Women*, p. 160. Nashville, TN: Nelson Books.

22. Metaxas, E. (2015). *7 Women*, p. 162. Nashville, TN: Nelson Books.

Week 3

23. Sproul, R.C. (1999) *In the Presence of God: Devotional Readings on the Attributes of God.* p.136. Nashville, TN: Thomas Nelson.

Week 4

24. Knowledge. (n.d.). *Merriam-Webster Dictionary.* Retrieved from https://www.merriam-Webster.com/dictionary/knowledge

25. Patterson, D., Kelley, R. (2011). *Women's Evangelical Commentary Old Testament*, p. 1044-1045. Nashville, TN: B&H Publishing Group.

26. Dermarest, B., Matthew, K. (2010). *Dictionary of Everyday Theology and Culture*, p. 171-172. Colorado Springs, CO: Navpress.

27. Patterson, D., Kelley, R. (2011). *Women's Evangelical Commentary Old Testament*, p. 13-14. Nashville, TN: B&H Publishing Group.

28. Dermarest, B., Matthews, K. (2010). *Dictionary of Everyday Theology and Culture*, p.365. Colorado Springs, CO: Navpress.

29. McGee, R. (1985). *The Search for Significance*, p. 140-141. Nashville, TN: Lifeway Christian Resources.

30. Hindson, E., Caner, E. (2008). *The Popular Encyclopedia of Apologetics*, p. 498. Eugene, OR: Harvest House Publishers.

31. Hindson, E., Caner, E. (2008). The *Popular Encyclopedia of Apologetics,* p. 124-125. Eugene, OR: Harvest House Publishers.

32. Patterson, D., Kelley, R. (2006). *Women's Evangelical Commentary New Testament*, p. 609. Nashville, TN: Broadman and Holman Publishers.

33. Patterson, D., Kelley, R. (2006). *Women's Evangelical Commentary New Testament*, p. 714. Nashville, TN: Broadman and Holman Publishers.

34. Wiersbe, W. (1989). *The Bible Exposition Commentary*, p. 2438. Wheaton, IL: SP Publications, Inc.

35. Wiersbe, W. (1989). *The Bible Exposition Commentary*, p. 758. Wheaton, IL: SP Publications, Inc.

Week 5

36. Guyon, J. (2001). *Madame Jeanne Guyon*, p. 13, Gainesville, FL: Bridge-Logos.

37. Keller, T. (2014). *Prayer: Experiencing Awe and Intimacy with God*, p. 17. New York, NY: Penguin Books.

38. Chambers, O. (2010). *If You Will Ask: Reflections on the Power of Prayer*, p. 8. Grand Rapids, MI: Discovery House Publishing.

39. Keller, T. (2014). *Prayer: Experiencing Awe and Intimacy with God*, p. 23. New York, NY: Penguin Books.

40. Carre, E. G. (1982) *Praying Hyde, Apostle of Prayer: The Life and Story of John Hyde*, p. 78. Alachua, FL: Bridge-Logos.

41. Augustine, S. (1960) *The Confessions of St. Augustine*, p. 92. NewYork, NY: Doubleday.

42. Bounds, E. M. (1997) *E. M. Bounds on Prayer*, p. 477. New Kensington, PA: Whitaker House.

43. Keller, T. (2014). *Prayer: Experiencing Awe and Intimacy with God*, p. 23. New York, NY: Penguin Books.

Week 6

44. Thompson, W. Oscar. (1999). *Concentric Circles of Concern*, p. 72. Nashville, TN: Broadman & Holman Publishers.

45. Abide. Wisdom. (n.d.). *Merriam-Webster Dictionary*. Retrieved from https://www.merriam-webster.com/dictionary/abide

46. Thompson, W. Oscar. (1999). *Concentric Circles of Concern*, p. 73. Nashville, TN: Broadman & Holman Publishers.

47. Gire, K. (1998) *Moments with the Savior*, p. 412. Grand Rapid, MI: Zondervan.

48. Warren, R. (2017). *The Definition of Joy – Daily Hope with Rick Warren – May 21, 2017*. http://pastorrick.com/devotional/english/the-definition-of-joy.

49. Gire, K. (1998). *Moments with the Savior*, p. 412. Grand Rapids, MI: Zondervan.

50. Clarkson, S. (2014). *Own Your Life*, p. 191. Carol Stream, IL: Tyndale House Publishers, Inc.

51. Sproul, R.C. (2004). Tabletalk Magazine. *The Fruit of Patience – September 1, 2004*. http://www.ligonier.org/learn/articles/fruit-patience/.

52. Rogers, A. (2016). *Kindness in the Home – June 21, 2016*. https://www.lwf.org/daily-treasures/posts/kindness-in-the-home.

53. Rogers, A. (2016). *Too Busy to be Kind – June 20, 2016*. https://www.lwf.org/daily-treasures/posts/too-busy-to-be-kind-2.

54. Goodness. (n.d.). *Merriam-Webster Dictionary*. Retrieved from https://www.merriam-webster.com/dictionary/goodness

55. *Life Application Study Bible, New Living Translation*, p. 1598. (2007). Carol Stream, IL: Tyndale House Publishers, Inc.

56. Straub, J. (2011). *Finding Goodness*. http://www.focusonthefamily.com/parenting/spiritual-growth-for-kids/fruit-of-the-spirit/finding-goodness.

57. Lewis, C.S. (1980). *Mere Christianity*, p. 141. New York, NY: HarperCollins Publishers, Inc.

58. Bruner, K. (2011). *Reflecting God's Faithfulness*. http://www.focusonthefamily.com/parenting/spiritual-growth-for-kids/fruit-of-the-spirit/reflecting-gods-faithfulness.

59. Strauss, Richard L. (2004). *Great is Thy Faithfulness*. https://bible.org/seriespage/23-great-thy-faithfulness.

60. Thomas, G. (2011). *Strength of Gentleness*. https://www.focusonthefamily.com/parenting/spiritual-growth-for-kids/fruit-of-the-spirit/strength-of-gentleness.

61. Lucado, M. (1994). *When God Whispers Your Name*, p. 73. Nashville, TN: Thomas Nelson.

62. Piper, John. (May 15, 2017). *What Is Meekness*. https://www.desiringgod.org/articles/what-is-meekness.

Week 7

63. Patterson, D., Kelley, R. (2011). *Women's Evangelical Commentary Old Testament*, p. 8. Nashville, TN: B&H Publishing Group.

64. Strauch, A. (1999) *Men and Women Equal Yet Different*, p. 23. Colorado Springs, CO: Lewis and Roth Publishers.

65. Kassian, M., Demoss, N. (2012). *Divine Design*, p. 94. Chicago, IL: Moody Publishers.

66. Kassian, M., Demoss, N. (2012). *Divine Design*, p. 107. Chicago, IL: Moody Publishers.

67. Kassian, M., Demoss, N. (2012). *Divine Design*, p. 109. Chicago, IL: Moody Publishers.

68. Kassian, M., Demoss, N. (2012). *Divine Design*, p. 126. Chicago, IL: Moody Publishers.

69. Kassian, M., Demoss, N. (2012). *Divine Design*, p. 134. Chicago, IL: Moody Publishers.

70. Pipers, J., Grudum, W. (1991). *Recovering Biblical Manhood and Womanhood*, p. 73. Wheaton, IL: Crossway Books.

71. Patterson, D., Kelley, R. (2011). *Women's Evangelical Commentary Old Testament*, p. 12-13. Nashville, TN: B&H Publishing Group.

72. Lenow, E., (2013). *Biblically Correct: Engaging Culture with Truth*, p. 53. Blog at Wordpress.com.

73. Lenow, E., (2013). *Biblically Correct: Engaging Culture with Truth*, p. 53. Blog at Wordpress.com.

74. Piper, J., Grudum, W. (1991). *Recovering Biblical Manhood and Womanhood*, p. 61. Wheaton, IL: Crossway Books.

75. Wiersbe, W. (1989). *The Bible Exposition Commentary*, p. 51. Wheaton, IL: SP Publications, Inc.

76. Eggerichs, E. (2004) *Love & Respect*, p. 18. Nashville, TN: Thomas Nelson.

77. Mahoney, C. (2003) *Feminine Appeal*, p.138. Wheaton, IL: Crossway.

78. Mahoney, C. (2003) *Feminine Appeal*, p.139. Wheaton, IL: Crossway.

79. Kassian, M., Demoss, N. (2012). *Devine Design*, p.140. Chicago, IL: Moody Publishers.

80. Strauch, A. (1999) *Men and Women Equal Yet Different*, p. 6-8. Colorado Springs, CO: Lewis and Roth Publishers.

81. Piper, J., Grudum, W. (1991). *Recovering Biblical Manhood and Womanhood*, p. 70. Wheaton, IL: Crossway Books.

82. Kassian, M., Demoss, N. (2012). *Divine Design*, p. 17. Chicago, IL: Moody Publishers.

Week 8

83. Thompson, W. Oscar. (1999). *Concentric Circles of Concern*, p. 91. Nashville, TN: Broadman & Holman Publishers.

84. Tozer, A.W. (2006). *The Pursuit of God*, p. 30-32. Chicago, IL: Moody Bible Institute of Chicago.

85. Warren, Rick. (2017). *What Forgiveness Really Is – Daily Hope with Rick Warren – April 13, 2016*. www. crosswalk.com.

86. Logan, Jim. (1995). *Reclaiming Surrendered Ground*, p. 70. Chicago, IL: Moody Publishers.

87. Kraft, Vickie. (2007). *Lesson 7: A Disease Called Unforgiveness*.

88. *Edens Structural Solutions*. (2017). Retrieved from https://edensstructural.com/when-trees-attack-how-tree-roots-damage-your-foundation/.

89. Kraft, Vickie. (2007). *Lesson 7: A Disease Called Unforgiveness*. https://bible.org/seriespage/lesson-7-disease-called-unforgiveness.

90. *Life Application Study Bible, New Living Translation*, p. 1153. (2007). Carol Stream, IL: Tyndale House Publishers, Inc.

91. Cole, Steven J. (2013). *Psalm 32: The Blessings of Obedience*. https://bible.org/seriespage/psalm-32-blessings-forgiveness.

92. Cole, Steven J. (2013). *Psalm 32: The Blessings of Obedience*. https://bible.org/seriespage/psalm-32-blessings-forgiveness.

93. Calvin, J. (2009). *John Calvin's Commentary on the Psalms*, p.362. Altenmuster, Germany: Jazzybee-Verlag.

94. Kimmel. T., (2006) *Grace-Based Marriage*. Video. Brentwood, TN: Worthy Publishing.

95. *Life Application Study Bible, New Living Translation*, p. 123. (2007). Carol Stream, IL:Tyndale House Publishers, Inc.

96. Warren, Rick. (2017). *The Cross Says 'Let It Go' – Daily Hope with Rick Warren – April 14, 2017*. http://pastorrick.com/devotional/english/full-post/the-cross-says-let-it-go.

Week 10

97. Barclay, W. (1975). *The Gospel of Matthew*, p. 280. Louisville, KY: Westminster John Knox Press.

98. Self-Discipline. (n.d.) *Cambridge Dictionary*. Retrieved from https://dictionary.cambridge.org/us/dictionary/english/self-discipline

99. Egkrateia. (n.d.). *Bible Study Tools*. Retrieved from https://www.biblestudytools.com/lexicons/greek/nas/egkrateia.html

100. Maxwell, J.C. (2017). *The Power of Significance: How Purpose Changes Your Life*, p. 57. New York, NY: Hatchette Book Group.

101. Roosevelt, T. (n.d.). *AZ Quotes*. Retrieved from http://www.azquotes.com/quote/1056535

102. *Life Application Study Bible, New Living Translation,* p.656. (1996). Carol Stream, IL: Tyndale House Publishing.

103. Welch, E. (2001). Self-Control: The Battle Against "One More". *The Journal of Biblical Counseling, 19*(2), 30.

104. Chambers, O. (2000). *My Utmost for His Highest (December 10),* p. 251. Uhrichsville, OH: Barbour Publishing.

105. Ortberg, J. (2002, July) Ruthlessly Eliminate Hurry. *Christianity Today Leadership Journal Online.* Retrieved from http://www.christianitytoday.com/pastors/2002/july-online-only/cln20704.html

106. Tozer, A.W. (1961). *Knowledge of the Holy,* pp. 46-47. San Francisco, CA: Harper Collins.

107. Fenelon, F. (2008). *The Complete Fenelon,* pp. 187-188. Brewster, MA: Paraclete Press.

108. Than, K. (2010, June). *National Geographic.* Retrieved from https://news.nationalgeographic.com/2010/06/100603-science-guatemala-sinkhole-2010-humans-caused/

109. Twain, M. (n.d.). *Brainy Quote.* Retrieved from https://www.brainyquote.com/quotes/mark_twain_414009

110. Rohn, J. (n.d.). 17 Remarkable Quotes by Jim Rohn. *Success.* https://www.success.com/article/17-remarkable-quotes-by-jim-rohn

111. Batterson, M. (2013). *All In,* p. 171. Grand Rapids, MI: Zondervan.

112. Batterson, M. (2013). *All In,* p. 171. Grand Rapids, MI: Zondervan.

113. Batterson, M. (2013). *All In,* pp. 171-172. Grand Rapids, MI: Zondervan.

114. Franklin, B. (2012). *Poor Richard's Almanac,* p. 20. New York, NY: Renaissance Classics.

115. Wooden, J. (1997). *Wooden: A Lifetime of Observations and Reflections On and Off the Court,* p.11. New York, NY: McGraw-Hill.

116. Regula. (n.d.). *Latin Dictionary.* Retrieved from http://www.latin-dictionary.net/search/latin/regula

117. All. (n.d.). *Merriam-Webster Dictionary.* Retrieved from https://www.merriam-webster.com/dictionary/all

118. Ortberg, J. *The Life You've Always Wanted,* p. 201. Grand Rapids, MI: Zondervan.

119. Laubach, R. S. (2007). *Letters by a Modern Mystic,* p. 14. Colorado Springs, CO: Purposeful Designs.

120. Peterson, E. (2000). *A Long Obedience in the Same Direction,* p. 5. Downer's Grove, IL: InterVarsity Press

121. Peterson, E. (2000). *A Long Obedience in the Same Direction*, p. 5. Downer's Grove, IL: InterVarsity Press.

Week 11

122. Heschel, Abraham Joshua and Susannah. (1951). *The Sabbath: Its Meaning for Modern Man*, p. 10-11. New York, NY: Farrar, straus, Giroux.

123. Shirer, Priscilla. (2014). *Breathe: Making Room for Sabbath*, p. 15. Nashville, TN: LifeWay Press.

124. Cole, Steven J. (2013). *God's Day of Rest*. https://bible.org/seriespage/lesson-5-god-s- day-rest-genesis-21-3.

125. *The Spurgeon Study Bible, CSB*, p. 98-99. (2017). Nashville, TN: Holman Bible Publishers.

126. Ortberg, John. (2002). *The Life You've Always Wanted*, p. 77. Grand Rapids, MI: Zondervan.

127. Ortberg, John. (2002). *The Life You've Always Wanted*, p. 79. Grand Rapids, MI: Zondervan Ibid, p. 79.

128. *The Spurgeon Study Bible, CSB*, p. 1336. (2017). Nashville, TN: Holman Bible Publishers.

129. Sorge, Bob. (2017). *Secrets of the Secret Place*, p. 61. Kansas City, MO: Oasis House.

130. Ortberg, John. (2002). *The Life You've Always Wanted*, p. 83. Grand Rapids, MI: Zondervan.

131. Shirer, Priscilla. (2014). *Breathe: Making Room for Sabbath*, p. 89. Nashville, TN: LifeWay Press.

132. Marginalize. (n.d.). Merriam-Webster Dictionary. Retrieved from https://www.merriam-webster.com/dictionary/marginalize

133. Shirer, Priscilla. (2014). *Breathe: Making Room for Sabbath*, p. 108. Nashville, TN: LifeWay Press.

134. Warren, Rick. (2014). Hear God: Eliminate the Distractions – *Daily Hope with Rick Warren – May 21, 2014*. http://pastorrick.com/devotional/english/hear-god-eliminate-the-distractions.

135. Third Day, *Your Words*.

136. Lucado, Max. (2017). *Anxious for Nothing: Finding Calm in a Chaotic World*, p. 6, 8. Nashville, TN: Thomas Nelson.

137. Lucado, Max. (2017). *Anxious for Nothing: Finding Calm in a Chaotic World*, p. 6. Nashville, TN: Thomas Nelson.

138. Lucado, Max. (2017). *Anxious for Nothing: Finding Calm in a Chaotic World*, p. 6. Nashville, TN: Thomas Nelson.

139. Lucado, Max. (2017). *Anxious for Nothing: Finding Calm in a Chaotic World*, p. 6. Nashville, TN: Thomas Nelson.

140. Lucado, Max. (2017). *Anxious for Nothing: Finding Calm in a Chaotic World*, p. 6. Nashville, TN: Thomas Nelson.

141. Lucado, Max. (2017). *Anxious for Nothing: Finding Calm in a Chaotic World*, p. 8. Nashville, TN: Thomas Nelson.

142. Lucado, Max. (2017). *Anxious for Nothing: Finding Calm in a Chaotic World*, p. 32. Nashville, TN: Thomas Nelson.

143. Warren, Rick. (2016). *Building Margin into Your Life – Daily Hope with Rick Warren – Oct. 7, 2016.* http://pastorrick.com/devotional/english/building-margin-into-your-life.

144. Lucado, Max. (2017). *Anxious for Nothing: Finding Calm in a Chaotic World*, p. 10. Nashville, TN: Thomas Nelson.

145. Lucado, Max. (2017). *Anxious for Nothing: Finding Calm in a Chaotic World*, p. 10. Nashville, TN: Thomas Nelson.

146. Lucado, Max. (2017). *Anxious for Nothing: Finding Calm in a Chaotic World*, p. 10. Nashville, TN: Thomas Nelson.

147. Lucado, Max. (2017). *Anxious for Nothing: Finding Calm in a Chaotic World*, p. 10. Nashville, TN: Thomas Nelson.

148. Shirer, Priscilla. (2014). *Breathe: Making Room for Sabbath*, p. 110. Nashville, TN: LifeWay Press.

149. Spurgeon, C. (2016). *Till He Come*, p. 109. Dallas, TX: Gideon House Books.

Week 12

150. Strauch, A. (1993). *The Hospitality Commands*, p.6. Littleton, CO: Lewis & Roth Publishers.

151. Piper, John. Strategic Hospitality. *Desiring God*. Retrieved from https://www.desiringgod.org/messages/strategic-hospitality

152. Cronkhite, R. (2003). *A Return to Sunday Dinner*, p. 195. Sisters, OR: Multnomah.

153. Lucado, M. (2010). *Outlive Your Life*, p. 55. Nashville, TN: Thomas Nelson Publishers.

154. Clarkson, S. & Clarkson, S. (2015). *The Life Giving Home*, p. 26. Carol Stream, IL: Tyndale House Publishing.

155. Mains, K. (1976). *Open Heart, Open Home*, p. 26. Elgin, IL: David C. Cook Publishing.

156. Warren, R. (2012). *The Purpose Driven Life*, p. 190. Grand Rapids, MI: Zondervan.

157. Willis, D. & Clements, B. (2017). *The Simplest Way to Change the World: Biblical Hospitality as a Way of Life*, pp. 40-41. Chicago, IL: Moody Publishers.

158. Clarkson, S. & Clarkson, S. (2015). *The Life Giving Home*, p. 26. Carol Stream, IL: Tyndale House Publishing.

159. Clarkson, S. & Clarkson, S. (2015). *The Life Giving Home*, p. 25. Carol Stream, IL: Tyndale House Publishing.

160. Piper, John. Strategic Hospitality. *Desiring God*. Retrieved from https://www.desiringgod.org/messages/strategic-hospitality

161. *International Standard Bible Encyclopedia*. (n.d.) Retrieved from https://www.biblestudytools.com/encyclopedias/isbe/

162. Strauch, A. (1993). *The Hospitality Commands*, p. 16. Littleton, CO: Lewis & Roth Publishers.

163. Ennis, P. & Tatlock, L. (2007). *Practicing Hospitality*, p. 50. Wheaton, IL: Crossway Books.

164. Willis, D. & Clements, B. (2017). *The Simplest Way to Change the World: Biblical Hospitality as a Way of Life*, p. 93. Chicago, IL: Moody Publishers.

165. Foster, J. (n.d.). *Christian Hospitality a Way of Life*. Retrieved from http://faithepchurch.org/files/Documents/Discipleship%20Resources/Hospitality.pdf

166. Philozenia. *Vine's Expository Dictionary of Biblical Words*.

167. Unger, M. (1961). *Unger's Bible Dictionary*, p. 502. Chicago, IL: Moody Publishers.

168. Freeman, J. (1972). *Manners and Customs of the Bible*, pp. 16-17. Plainfield, NJ: Logos International.

169. Strauch, A. (1993). *The Hospitality Commands*, p. 24. Littleton, CO: Lewis & Roth Publishers.

170. Nouwen, H. (1975). *Reaching Out: The Three Movements of the Spiritual Life*, p. 65. New York, NY: Doubleday.

171. Maxwell, J. (2015). *Intentional Living: Choosing a Life That Matters*, p. 30. New York, NY: Hatchette Book Group.

172. Strauch, A. (1993). *The Hospitality Commands*, pp. 37-38. Littleton, CO: Lewis & Roth Publishers.

82944122R00141